Zoom Meeting Essentials

A Step-by-Step Guide

Kiet Huynh

Table of Contents

CHAPTER I Getting Started with Zoom 6

1.1 Introduction to Zoom..6

    1.1.1 What is Zoom?...6

    1.1.2 Why Use Zoom for Meetings? 11

    1.1.3 Free vs. Paid Plans...16

1.2 Setting Up Your Zoom Account 22

    1.2.1 Creating an Account...22

    1.2.2 Navigating the Zoom Dashboard..28

    1.2.3 Understanding User Roles and Permissions................................35

1.3 Installing Zoom on Different Devices 41

    1.3.1 Installing Zoom on Windows and Mac...41

    1.3.2 Using Zoom on Mobile (iOS and Android) 46

    1.3.3 Zoom Web Client vs. Zoom Desktop App....................................51

CHAPTER II Hosting and Joining Meetings...57

2.1 Scheduling a Zoom Meeting...57

    2.1.1 How to Schedule a Meeting 57

    2.1.2 Setting Up Recurring Meetings 64

    2.1.3 Time Zone and Calendar Integration 68

2.2 Joining a Zoom Meeting...75

    2.2.1 Joining via Link or Meeting ID..75

    2.2.2 Troubleshooting Common Joining Issues 80

2.3 Starting and Managing a Meeting 86

    2.3.1 Starting an Instant Meeting...86

    2.3.2 Enabling Waiting Rooms and Passcodes 93

    2.3.3 Managing Participants..99

CHAPTER III Using Zoom Meeting Features 107

3.1 Audio and Video Controls 107

   3.1.1 Adjusting Microphone and Speaker Settings 107

   3.1.2 Managing Video Settings and Backgrounds.........................113

   3.1.3 Muting and Unmuting Participants 119

3.2 Screen Sharing and Presenting..126

   3.2.1 Sharing Your Screen..126

   3.2.2 Optimizing Video and Audio for Presentations..................132

3.3 Chat, Reactions, and Polling 137

   3.3.1 Sending Messages in Chat..137

   3.3.2 Using Emojis and Reactions..143

   3.3.3 Creating and Managing Polls..149

CHAPTER IV Advanced Zoom Features...157

4.1 Breakout Rooms for Group Discussions 157

   4.1.1 Setting Up Breakout Rooms..157

   4.1.2 Assigning Participants Manually vs. Automatically 162

   4.1.3 Managing Breakout Sessions 167

4.2 Recording and Transcription...173

   4.2.1 How to Record a Meeting..173

   4.2.2 Local vs. Cloud Recording...178

   4.2.3 Using Live Transcription and Subtitles 183

4.3 Security and Privacy Settings..189

   4.3.1 Enabling End-to-End Encryption 189

   4.3.2 Managing Meeting Permissions.......................................192

   4.3.3 Handling Zoombombing and Unwanted Guests 196

CHAPTER V Best Practices for Effective Zoom Meetings......................201

5.1 Preparing for a Professional Meeting...201

   5.1.1 Optimizing Lighting and Background.................................201

5.1.2 Choosing the Right Audio Setup 206

5.1.3 Setting Up an Agenda...211

5.2 Engaging Participants..217

5.2.1 Encouraging Interaction and Participation 217

5.2.2 Using Visual Aids Effectively..222

5.2.3 Managing Q&A Sessions 227

5.3 Troubleshooting Common Issues..232

5.3.1 Dealing with Connection and Audio Problems.........................232

5.3.2 Handling Video and Screen Freezing Issues.............................236

5.3.3 Fixing Zoom Crashes and Errors 241

CHAPTER VI Zoom for Different Use Cases **246**

6.1 Zoom for Business and Team Collaboration 246

6.1.1 Hosting Webinars and Large Meetings.....................................246

6.1.2 Using Zoom for Remote Team Meetings 250

6.1.3 Integrating Zoom with Slack and Microsoft Teams.................255

6.2 Zoom for Education and Online Learning...260

6.2.1 Engaging Students with Interactive Features...........................260

6.2.2 Managing Virtual Classrooms 264

6.2.3 Recording and Sharing Lectures...268

6.3 Zoom for Personal Use and Social Gatherings 274

6.3.1 Virtual Family Meetings and Celebrations...............................274

6.3.2 Hosting Online Events and Parties 279

6.3.3 Using Zoom for Fitness and Hobby Groups 284

Conclusion **290**

7.1 Recap of Key Zoom Features 290

7.1.1 Essential Tools for Effective Meetings...**290**

Acknowledgments 294

CHAPTER I
Getting Started with Zoom

1.1 Introduction to Zoom

1.1.1 What is Zoom?

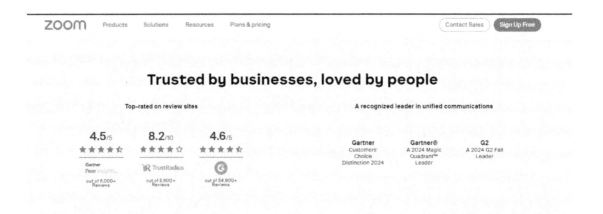

Introduction

Zoom is a widely used video conferencing software that enables individuals and businesses to communicate virtually through video calls, voice calls, and instant messaging. It has become one of the most popular platforms for remote work, online education, virtual events, and personal communication. Whether you need to hold a team meeting, teach an online class, or simply catch up with friends and family, Zoom provides a reliable and feature-rich solution.

Since its launch in 2011, Zoom has grown exponentially, becoming a household name, especially after the COVID-19 pandemic accelerated the adoption of remote communication tools. With its user-friendly interface, high-quality video and audio, and a wide range of collaboration features, Zoom has revolutionized the way people connect across the world.

History and Development of Zoom

Zoom Video Communications was founded in 2011 by Eric Yuan, a former lead engineer at Cisco WebEx, with the goal of creating a better video conferencing solution. Yuan believed that existing video conferencing software was complex, unreliable, and did not meet the needs of modern users. He envisioned a simple, seamless, and efficient platform that would allow people to communicate without technical difficulties.

Zoom officially launched its platform in 2013 and quickly gained traction among businesses, educators, and individuals. The company's focus on ease of use, scalability, and superior video quality helped it stand out in a competitive market. By 2019, Zoom had become one of the top video conferencing platforms in the world, and its user base surged dramatically in 2020 due to the global shift to remote work and online learning.

Key Features of Zoom

Zoom offers a comprehensive set of features designed to enhance virtual communication. Below are some of the key functionalities that make Zoom an industry leader in video conferencing:

1. High-Quality Video and Audio

Zoom provides HD video and audio, ensuring clear and professional communication. Users can adjust their video resolution based on their internet bandwidth to maintain a smooth experience.

2. Screen Sharing

One of the most valuable features of Zoom is the ability to share your screen with other participants. This is useful for presentations, training sessions, and remote collaboration. Users can choose to share their entire screen or a specific window.

3. Virtual Backgrounds and Filters

Zoom allows users to customize their video background with virtual images or blur effects. This feature is particularly useful for maintaining privacy and creating a professional appearance.

4. Meeting Recording

Zoom enables users to record meetings, either locally on their computer or in the cloud. This feature is beneficial for those who need to review meetings later or share them with colleagues who couldn't attend.

5. Breakout Rooms

Breakout rooms allow meeting hosts to divide participants into smaller groups for discussions or group activities. This feature is commonly used in online classrooms and business meetings.

6. Chat and File Sharing

Zoom includes a built-in chat function where participants can send messages, links, and files during a meeting. This feature facilitates better communication and collaboration.

7. Webinar Capabilities

For large-scale events, Zoom offers webinar hosting, which allows hosts to broadcast to large audiences while maintaining control over participant interaction.

8. Integration with Third-Party Applications

Zoom integrates with various third-party applications, including Slack, Microsoft Teams, Google Drive, and Dropbox. These integrations help users streamline their workflow and improve productivity.

Who Uses Zoom?

Zoom is widely adopted across different industries and user groups, including:

1. Businesses and Corporations

Companies of all sizes use Zoom for virtual meetings, team collaboration, training sessions, and client interactions. Many businesses rely on Zoom to maintain seamless communication among remote teams.

2. Educational Institutions

Schools, colleges, and universities use Zoom for online learning, virtual classrooms, and student collaboration. Features like screen sharing, breakout rooms, and recording capabilities make it a valuable tool for educators.

3. Healthcare Industry

Doctors and healthcare providers use Zoom for telemedicine, allowing them to consult with patients remotely. Secure encryption and HIPAA compliance make Zoom a preferred choice for virtual medical consultations.

4. Government and Non-Profit Organizations

Governments and non-profit organizations use Zoom for public meetings, community outreach, and internal collaboration.

5. Personal and Social Use

Individuals use Zoom to stay connected with friends and family, host virtual parties, conduct online yoga sessions, and participate in hobby groups.

Zoom's Popularity and Growth

The COVID-19 pandemic significantly increased Zoom's user base, with millions of people worldwide relying on it for work, education, and social interactions. In April 2020, Zoom reported over **300 million daily meeting participants**, a drastic increase from just 10 million in December 2019.

Its rapid growth can be attributed to:

- **User-friendly interface** – Zoom is easy to set up and use, even for beginners.

- **Reliability and stability** – The platform provides smooth video and audio quality with minimal disruptions.

- **Flexible pricing plans** – Zoom offers both free and paid plans, making it accessible to everyone.

- **Cross-platform availability** – Zoom is available on Windows, Mac, iOS, Android, and web browsers.

Limitations and Challenges

Despite its many advantages, Zoom is not without its challenges. Some of the common issues users may face include:

1. Security and Privacy Concerns

In the early months of 2020, Zoom faced criticism for security vulnerabilities, including **Zoombombing**, where unauthorized users disrupted meetings. Since then, the company has implemented security enhancements, such as meeting passcodes, waiting rooms, and end-to-end encryption.

2. Internet Dependency

Zoom requires a stable internet connection for optimal performance. Users with slow or unstable internet may experience lag, audio dropouts, or disconnections.

3. Learning Curve for Advanced Features

While basic Zoom functions are easy to use, advanced features like breakout rooms, webinar hosting, and integrations may require some learning. However, Zoom provides extensive documentation and tutorials to help users.

Conclusion

Zoom has transformed the way people communicate and collaborate in the digital age. Its intuitive interface, high-quality video and audio, and powerful collaboration tools make it a top choice for businesses, educators, healthcare professionals, and individuals.

As remote work and online interactions continue to grow, Zoom remains a valuable tool for connecting people worldwide. Whether you are using Zoom for business, education, or personal connections, understanding its features and capabilities will help you maximize its potential and enhance your virtual communication experience.

What's Next?

Now that you understand what Zoom is and why it's so widely used, the next section will guide you through setting up your Zoom account and navigating its interface. Let's get started!

1.1.2 Why Use Zoom for Meetings?

Powering organizations across industries and geographies

Zoom helps consolidate communications, connect people, and collaborate better together in the boardroom, classroom, operating room, and everywhere in between.

Explore Industry Solutions

Introduction

In today's digital era, virtual communication has become a necessity for businesses, educators, and individuals alike. Whether you're working remotely, attending online classes, or catching up with friends and family, an efficient and reliable video conferencing tool is essential. **Zoom** has emerged as one of the most popular platforms for online meetings, thanks to its user-friendly interface, high-quality video and audio, and a host of powerful features that facilitate seamless communication.

But what makes Zoom stand out among the many video conferencing tools available? In this section, we will explore the key reasons why Zoom is an excellent choice for virtual meetings and why it has become the go-to platform for millions of users worldwide.

1. Ease of Use

Simple Setup and Intuitive Interface

One of Zoom's biggest advantages is its simplicity. Unlike many other video conferencing tools that require complex configurations, Zoom makes it easy for users to get started within minutes.

- Quick account creation: Signing up for Zoom is straightforward, requiring only an email address or integration with Google, Apple, or Facebook accounts.

- Minimal setup: Once installed, users can immediately start or join meetings without needing extensive technical knowledge.

- User-friendly interface: The interface is designed to be intuitive, making it easy for users to navigate the platform, schedule meetings, and manage settings.

Accessibility Across Devices

Zoom is available on a wide range of devices, ensuring that users can connect from anywhere. Whether you're using a desktop, laptop, tablet, or smartphone, you can join Zoom meetings effortlessly.

- Multi-platform compatibility: Zoom runs on Windows, macOS, iOS, Android, and even Linux.

- Web browser access: If you don't want to download the app, you can join meetings directly from a web browser.

- Seamless transition between devices: Users can start a meeting on one device and switch to another without interruptions.

2. High-Quality Video and Audio

A virtual meeting is only as good as its video and audio quality. Poor sound and choppy video can lead to miscommunication and frustration. Zoom provides high-definition (HD) video and crystal-clear audio, ensuring that participants can see and hear each other clearly.

HD Video with Multiple Layouts

Zoom offers HD video streaming and several layout options to enhance the meeting experience:

- Speaker view: Automatically highlights the active speaker.

- Gallery view: Displays multiple participants on the screen at once, ideal for team discussions.

- Pinning and spotlighting: Hosts can pin or spotlight specific participants to keep the focus on key speakers.

Advanced Audio Features

Zoom's audio capabilities are designed to minimize disruptions and improve clarity:

- Noise suppression: Reduces background noise such as typing, barking dogs, or traffic sounds.

- Echo cancellation: Prevents audio feedback and echo issues.

- Adjustable microphone settings: Allows users to tweak audio settings for the best experience.

3. Robust Security and Privacy Features

Security is a major concern for online meetings, especially for businesses and educational institutions. Zoom has implemented several security measures to protect users and prevent unauthorized access.

End-to-End Encryption

Zoom offers end-to-end encryption (E2EE) for meetings, ensuring that conversations remain private and cannot be intercepted by hackers.

Meeting Passcodes and Waiting Rooms

To prevent unauthorized access, Zoom provides:

- Meeting passcodes: Hosts can set passwords that participants must enter before joining.

- Waiting rooms: Allows hosts to screen participants before granting them access to the meeting.

Host Controls and Participant Management

Hosts have full control over their meetings, including the ability to:

- Mute or remove disruptive participants

- Lock the meeting to prevent new attendees
- Restrict screen sharing to prevent unwanted content

4. Versatile Features for Different Meeting Types

Zoom is highly versatile, catering to a wide range of use cases, including business meetings, webinars, online classes, and social gatherings.

Business and Corporate Meetings

Companies use Zoom for team collaboration, client meetings, and remote work. Features like screen sharing, virtual backgrounds, and integrations with project management tools make it ideal for professional use.

Webinars and Online Events

Zoom's Webinar feature allows hosts to broadcast events to a large audience, with options for Q&A, live polling, and attendee engagement.

Education and Online Learning

Zoom is widely used in virtual classrooms, offering features like:

- Breakout rooms for small group discussions
- Whiteboard and annotation tools for interactive lessons
- Recording options for students to review later

Personal and Social Use

Beyond work and education, Zoom is also popular for virtual family gatherings, online fitness classes, and social events.

5. Scalability and Cost-Effectiveness

Free vs. Paid Plans

One of Zoom's key benefits is its flexible pricing structure.

- **Free Plan:**

- Host unlimited 1-on-1 meetings
- Group meetings up to 40 minutes
- Basic features like screen sharing and virtual backgrounds

- **Pro and Business Plans:**
  - Remove the 40-minute limit
  - Support for larger audiences
  - Additional features like cloud recording, reporting, and integrations

Works for Small and Large Organizations

Whether you're an individual, a small business, or a multinational corporation, Zoom can scale to fit your needs.

- Small businesses benefit from cost-effective plans and essential collaboration tools.
- Large enterprises can integrate Zoom with existing workflows and IT systems.

6. Integration with Other Tools

Zoom enhances productivity by seamlessly integrating with many third-party applications, including:

- Google Calendar & Outlook – Schedule and manage meetings effortlessly.
- Slack & Microsoft Teams – Launch Zoom calls directly from chat platforms.
- Trello & Asana – Connect with project management tools for better collaboration.

These integrations help teams streamline communication and workflow efficiency.

Conclusion

Zoom has revolutionized the way people communicate, offering a reliable, secure, and feature-rich platform for virtual meetings. Whether you're a business professional, a teacher, or someone looking to stay connected with family and friends, Zoom provides an easy-to-use and high-quality solution for online communication.

With its HD video and audio, strong security features, scalability, and powerful integrations, Zoom remains one of the best choices for online meetings. As we continue to adapt to a digital-first world, mastering Zoom can boost productivity, improve collaboration, and enhance communication in both personal and professional settings.

By leveraging the capabilities of Zoom, users can host engaging, efficient, and secure virtual meetings, ensuring that distance is no longer a barrier to effective communication.

1.1.3 Free vs. Paid Plans

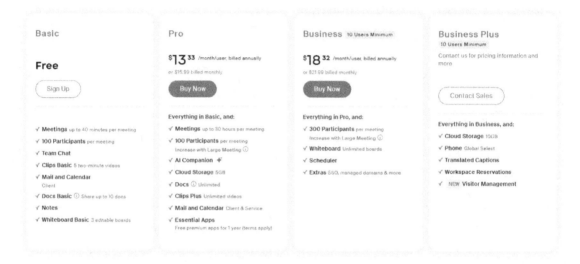

Zoom offers a variety of pricing plans to accommodate different users, from individuals hosting occasional meetings to large enterprises requiring extensive collaboration tools. Understanding the differences between the **free (Basic)** and **paid (Pro, Business, and Enterprise)** plans is essential to choosing the right option for your needs.

This section will provide a detailed breakdown of what each plan offers, their limitations, and how to decide which one best suits your use case.

1. Free (Basic) Plan

The **Basic** plan is Zoom's free-tier option, designed primarily for individuals, small teams, and casual users. Despite being free, it provides a robust set of features suitable for most standard video conferencing needs.

Key Features of the Free Plan:

- **Unlimited one-on-one meetings** – You can have private meetings with another participant for as long as you like.

- **Up to 100 participants per meeting** – Suitable for small group meetings.

- **40-minute time limit for group meetings** – Meetings with three or more participants are automatically disconnected after 40 minutes.

- **Screen sharing** – Share your screen with participants for presentations, demos, or collaborations.

- **Virtual backgrounds** – Use Zoom's built-in virtual backgrounds to hide your surroundings.

- **In-meeting chat** – Send messages to all participants or privately chat with individuals.

- **Breakout rooms** – Divide participants into smaller groups for discussions.

- **Basic security features** – Includes passcodes, waiting rooms, and participant management controls.

Limitations of the Free Plan:

While the free plan is suitable for casual use, it comes with some restrictions that may make it less viable for professional or large-scale usage:

- **40-minute meeting limit** – Once the time limit is reached, the meeting ends automatically, requiring participants to reconnect.

- **Limited cloud recording** – No access to Zoom's cloud storage for saving meeting recordings (local recording is available, but only on computers).

- **No live transcription** – Automatic captions are not available, making accessibility harder.

- **Limited customer support** – Basic online support is available, but there's no live chat or dedicated support for technical issues.

The free plan is **best suited for** personal use, student group projects, or quick business calls that don't exceed the time limit.

---

2. Zoom Pro Plan

The **Pro** plan is Zoom's first paid tier, designed for small businesses, educators, and professionals who require extended meeting durations and additional features.

Key Features of the Pro Plan:

- **Increases meeting duration to 30 hours** – Allows for long and uninterrupted meetings.

- **Cloud recording (up to 5 GB of storage)** – Store meeting recordings in the cloud for easy access and sharing.

- **Live transcription** – Generates automatic captions for improved accessibility.

- **Polling and Q&A** – Enhance engagement with interactive polls.

- **Advanced meeting reports** – Get insights into attendee engagement and participation.

- **Streaming to social media** – Broadcast meetings directly to Facebook or YouTube.

- **Basic integrations** – Connect Zoom with productivity tools like Google Calendar, Slack, and Dropbox.

Limitations of the Pro Plan:

- **Still limited to 100 participants** (additional licenses required for more).

- **Limited cloud storage (5GB)** – May not be sufficient for users who record frequently.

- **No advanced branding or enterprise-grade security features.**

The Pro plan is **ideal for** small business owners, consultants, freelancers, and educators who need extended meetings and cloud recording.

---

3. Zoom Business Plan

The **Business** plan is designed for small and medium-sized businesses that need greater control, branding options, and more participant capacity.

Key Features of the Business Plan:

- **Up to 300 participants per meeting** – Ideal for growing teams.

- **Custom branding** – Add your company logo and customize emails and meeting links.

- **Admin dashboard and reporting** – Monitor usage, troubleshoot issues, and generate detailed reports.

- **Dedicated phone support** – Access to live customer service.

- **Advanced integrations** – Connect with third-party apps like Salesforce and Microsoft Teams.

- **Managed domains** – Secure your organization's Zoom accounts under a single domain.

Limitations of the Business Plan:

- **Still has a 30-hour meeting duration limit.**

- **Requires at least 10 user licenses** – Must purchase at least 10 accounts.

The Business plan is **ideal for** mid-sized companies, educational institutions, and organizations that need enhanced branding, security, and administrative control.

4. Zoom Enterprise Plan

The **Enterprise** plan is Zoom's highest-tier offering, designed for **large organizations** with advanced security needs and a high volume of meetings.

Key Features of the Enterprise Plan:

- **Up to 1,000 participants per meeting** – Perfect for corporate events and large-scale conferences.

- **Unlimited cloud storage** – No restrictions on how much meeting content you can save.

- **Priority customer support** – 24/7 dedicated technical support.

- **Advanced security and compliance** – Includes HIPAA compliance, encryption, and single sign-on (SSO) options.

- **Real-time analytics dashboard** – Track meeting metrics, user engagement, and system performance.

Limitations of the Enterprise Plan:

- **High cost** – The most expensive plan, making it suitable only for large organizations.

- **Requires at least 50 user licenses** – Not available for individuals or small businesses.

The Enterprise plan is **best suited for** large corporations, government agencies, universities, and multinational businesses that require large-scale collaboration and enhanced security.

5. Comparing All Plans: A Quick Summary

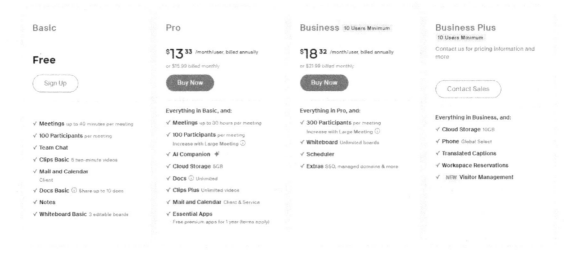

6. Choosing the Right Plan for Your Needs

- If you are an individual, student, or casual user, the Free plan is sufficient.

- If you need longer meetings, recording options, and transcription, the Pro plan is a good choice.

- If you are a small-to-medium business needing branding and admin tools, the Business plan is better.

- If you are a large company requiring enterprise-grade security and large meetings, the Enterprise plan is necessary.

Final Thoughts

Understanding Zoom's pricing structure and feature differences ensures you select the right plan for your needs. Whether you're a freelancer, business owner, or corporate executive, Zoom provides a plan that fits various collaboration requirements. Assess your meeting needs, budget, and team size before making a decision.

1.2 Setting Up Your Zoom Account

1.2.1 Creating an Account

Introduction

Before you can start using Zoom for virtual meetings, the first step is to create an account. Having a Zoom account allows you to schedule meetings, customize your settings, and access advanced features. Whether you are using Zoom for business, education, or personal use, creating an account is a simple process that takes only a few minutes.

This section will guide you through the process of creating a Zoom account, including signing up, verifying your email, setting up your profile, and configuring basic settings.

1. The Different Types of Zoom Accounts

Before signing up, it's important to understand the different types of Zoom accounts. Zoom offers multiple account tiers to accommodate various needs:

1.1 Basic (Free) Plan

- Allows unlimited one-on-one meetings.

- Group meetings (3 or more participants) have a **40-minute limit**.

- Includes essential features such as screen sharing, breakout rooms, and virtual backgrounds.

1.2 Pro Plan

- Removes the **40-minute limit** for group meetings.

- Offers **1 GB of cloud recording**.

- Includes additional features like meeting transcripts and polling.

1.3 Business Plan

- Designed for small to medium-sized businesses.

- Allows hosting of **up to 300 participants**.

- Provides **company branding** and administrative management tools.

1.4 Enterprise Plan

- Best for large organizations needing **advanced analytics** and security.

- Can host meetings with **500+ participants**.

- Provides **unlimited cloud storage** for recorded meetings.

Depending on your needs, you can start with a free account and later upgrade to a paid plan.

---

2. Step-by-Step Guide to Creating a Zoom Account

Creating a Zoom account is easy and can be done on both desktop and mobile devices.

2.1 Signing Up for a Zoom Account on a Web Browser

1. **Go to the Zoom website**
   - Open your web browser and navigate to https://zoom.us/signup.
   - You will be prompted to enter your **email address**.

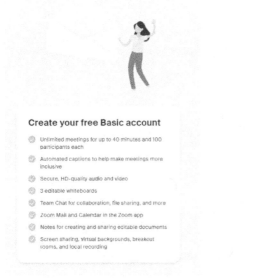

Create your free Basic account

- Unlimited meetings for up to 40 minutes and 100 participants each
- Automated captions to help make meetings more inclusive
- Secure, HD-quality audio and video
- 3 editable whiteboards
- Team Chat for collaboration, file sharing, and more
- Zoom Mail and Calendar in the Zoom app
- Notes for creating and sharing editable documents
- Screen sharing, virtual backgrounds, breakout rooms, and local recording

Let's Get Started

Email Address

Birth Year

Continue

By proceeding, I agree to Zoom's Privacy Statement and Terms of Service.

Or sign up with

SSO   Apple   Google   Facebook

Zoom is protected by reCAPTCHA and the Privacy Policy and Terms of Service apply.

2. **Choose Your Sign-Up Method**

   o You can sign up using:

      ▪ Your work email.

      ▪ Your Google account.

      ▪ Your Facebook account.

      ▪ Your SSO (Single Sign-On) method (for business users).

3. **Verify Your Email Address**

   o After entering your email, Zoom will send a verification link.

   o Check your inbox and click on the **confirmation link** to proceed.

   o If you don't receive an email, check your **spam folder** or request another email.

4. **Complete Your Profile**

   o After clicking the verification link, you'll be directed to Zoom's setup page.

   o Enter your **first and last name**.

   o Set a **strong password** (minimum 8 characters, including letters, numbers, and symbols).

5. **Skip or Invite Colleagues (Optional)**

   o Zoom may ask if you want to invite colleagues.

   o You can **skip this step** or enter emails to invite others.

6. **Access Your Account**

   o Once completed, you will be redirected to your **Zoom dashboard**.

2.2 Signing Up for a Zoom Account on Mobile

1. **Download the Zoom App**

   o Open the **App Store (iOS)** or **Google Play Store (Android)**.

- o   Search for **"Zoom Cloud Meetings"** and download the app.

2. **Launch the App**

    - o   Open the Zoom app and tap **Sign Up**.

3. **Enter Your Information**

    - o   Provide your email address, first name, and last name.

    - o   Agree to Zoom's Terms of Service.

4. **Verify Your Email**

    - o   Zoom will send a **confirmation email**.

    - o   Open your email, click on the verification link, and return to the app.

5. **Set Your Password**

    - o   Choose a **secure password** and confirm it.

6. **Log In to Your Account**

    - o   Use your email and password to **log in** and access the main Zoom interface.

3. Setting Up Your Zoom Profile

After creating an account, it's important to personalize your Zoom profile.

Updating Your Profile Picture

- Go to your **Zoom dashboard**.

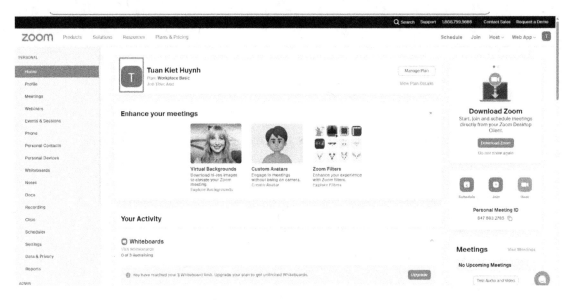

- Click **Profile** and select **Change Picture**.

- Upload a professional image (recommended for business users).

Setting Your Display Name

- Click **Edit** next to your name.

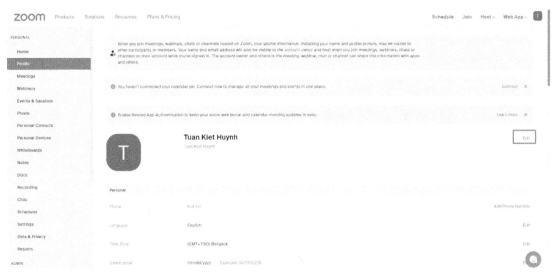

- Choose a display name that others will see in meetings.

Adding a Bio and Contact Information

- Some Zoom plans allow you to add a **short bio** and contact links.
- Useful for **networking and professional meetings**.

Troubleshooting Common Issues

Even though creating an account is simple, users may encounter issues.

Email Verification Issues

- **Check spam/junk folder** if you don't receive the confirmation email.
- **Resend verification email** from the Zoom signup page.

Login Issues

- If you **forgot your password**, use the **"Forgot Password"** option.
- Check if your **firewall or VPN** is blocking Zoom.

Account Restrictions

- Some corporate or school accounts have **admin restrictions**.
- Contact **your IT department** if you cannot create a personal Zoom account.

Final Tips for a Smooth Setup

- Use a **strong password** and keep your credentials secure.
- Customize your **profile picture and display name** for a professional appearance.
- Check and adjust **notification and meeting settings** before hosting meetings.
- Keep your Zoom app **updated** for the latest features and security fixes.

Conclusion

Creating a Zoom account is the first step toward using the platform for virtual communication. Whether you're using Zoom for professional meetings, online learning, or social gatherings, having a properly set up account ensures a seamless experience.

Once your account is created, you can explore additional settings and begin scheduling meetings. In the next section, we will discuss **navigating the Zoom dashboard** and **understanding user roles and permissions** to help you get the most out of Zoom.

✅ Key Takeaways

✓ Signing up for Zoom is **quick and easy** on both desktop and mobile.

✓ Verify your **email** and create a **strong password** for security.

✓ Customize your **profile** for a professional look.

✓ Adjust **settings** to optimize your experience before hosting meetings.

1.2.2 Navigating the Zoom Dashboard

Introduction

Once you have created a Zoom account, the next step is understanding the **Zoom Dashboard**—the central hub where you can manage meetings, settings, recordings, and more. Whether you are a casual user or an administrator managing a team, knowing how to navigate the Zoom Dashboard effectively will save you time and enhance your virtual meeting experience.

This section will provide a detailed **step-by-step guide** on accessing and using the Zoom Dashboard, covering its layout, key features, and customization options.

1. Understanding the Zoom Dashboard Layout

After logging into your Zoom account via https://zoom.us, you will be taken to the Zoom Dashboard. The Dashboard consists of several key sections:

Side Navigation Bar

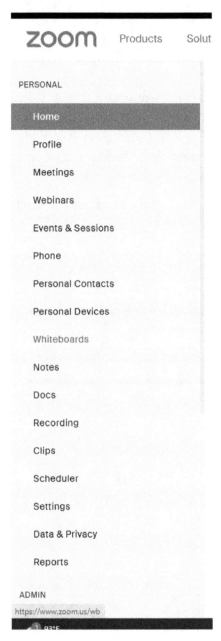

At the top of the Dashboard, you will find a navigation bar with quick access to various functions.

- **Profile**: View and edit personal account information.

- **Meetings**: Schedule, view, and manage upcoming and past meetings.

- **Webinars**: Manage scheduled webinars (available only with a Pro or Business plan).

- **Recordings**: Access and manage your local and cloud recordings.

- **Settings**: Adjust meeting settings, security preferences, and integrations.

- **Reports** (for admin users): View usage reports, meeting attendance, and other analytics.

- **Admin Controls** (for account owners/admins): Manage users, roles, and account-wide settings.

2. Key Features and Functions of the Zoom Dashboard

The Zoom Dashboard provides all the tools you need to manage your meetings efficiently. Below are its most important sections and how to use them effectively.

Profile Section

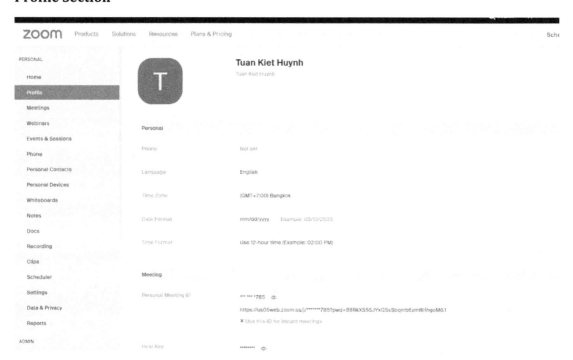

In the Profile section, you can manage your personal account details, including:

- Display Name & Profile Picture: Customize how your name appears in meetings.

- Sign-In Method: Set up login options such as email/password, Google, or Facebook login.

- Host Key: Manage your personal meeting room and security settings.

- Language & Time Zone: Adjust your preferred language and time zone settings.

- Subscription Plan: View your current Zoom plan and upgrade if needed.

Meetings Tab

The Meetings section is one of the most frequently used parts of the Dashboard. It allows you to:

- Schedule a Meeting: Set up one-time or recurring meetings with a unique Meeting ID.

- View Upcoming Meetings: Check all scheduled meetings and modify them if necessary.

- Start a Meeting: Begin an instant meeting or start a scheduled meeting.

- Manage Personal Meeting Room: Customize your permanent meeting room for quick access.

- Meeting Templates: Save meeting settings as templates for future use.

💡 Tip: If you frequently host meetings, pin this section in your browser for quick access.

Webinars Tab (For Pro/Business Users)

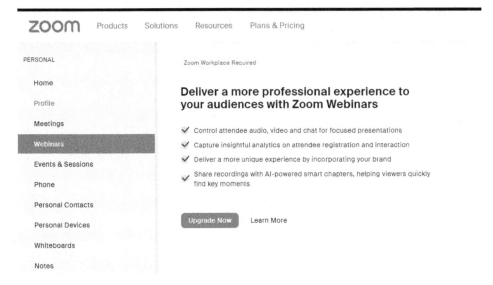

If you have a Pro, Business, or Enterprise Zoom plan, you can host webinars. The Webinars tab allows you to:

- Schedule Webinars with unique registration options.

- Manage Registrants and send automated reminders.

- Enable Q&A and Polling Features to engage participants.

- View Webinar Reports to track attendance and engagement.

Recordings Tab

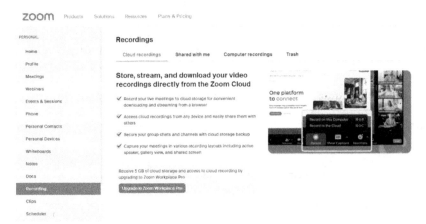

This section allows you to access and manage your local and cloud recordings.

- Local Recordings: View and manage recordings saved to your computer.

- Cloud Recordings (for Pro users): Store and share meeting recordings in the Zoom Cloud.

- Download & Share: Download recordings or generate shareable links.

- Automatic Transcripts: Enable transcription for recorded meetings.

💡 *Tip: If your cloud storage is limited, regularly download and delete old recordings.*

Settings Section

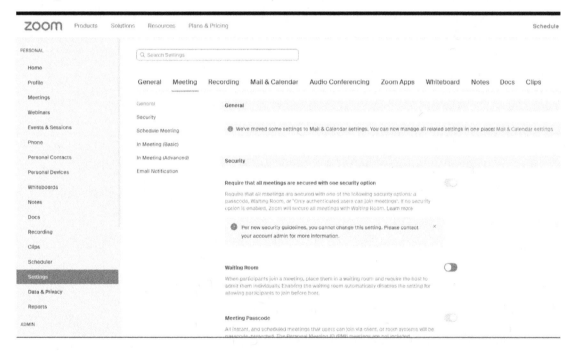

The Settings tab is one of the most powerful parts of the Zoom Dashboard. It allows you to customize:

- Meeting Security: Enable waiting rooms, passcodes, and authentication requirements.

- Audio & Video Settings: Configure microphone, camera, and virtual background options.

- Screen Sharing Permissions: Allow or restrict participants from sharing their screen.

- Recording Options: Set recording preferences and cloud storage limits.

- Chat & Reactions: Control chat availability, file sharing, and in-meeting reactions.

Reports Tab (For Admin Users)

For admins and hosts, the Reports tab provides valuable analytics about:

- Meeting Usage: Track how many meetings have been hosted.

- Participant Attendance: See who attended each meeting and for how long.

- Poll & Survey Results: View responses to in-meeting polls and surveys.

3. Customizing the Zoom Dashboard for Efficiency

Zoom allows you to personalize your Dashboard to optimize your workflow.

Enabling Shortcuts and Quick Actions

- Pin frequently used sections (Meetings, Recordings, etc.) in your browser.

- Use keyboard shortcuts to navigate faster (e.g., **Alt+U** for participants panel).

Integrating Zoom with Other Tools

You can integrate Zoom with:

- Google Calendar & Outlook for easy meeting scheduling.

- Slack & Microsoft Teams for seamless team communication.

- Zapier & Other Automation Tools to streamline workflows.

Managing Notifications & Alerts

- Set up email reminders for upcoming meetings.

- Enable push notifications on your mobile app.

- Customize recording alerts for automatic cloud uploads.

4. Troubleshooting Common Issues in the Zoom Dashboard

Even with an intuitive interface, users sometimes face technical difficulties in the Zoom Dashboard. Here's how to resolve common problems:

Unable to Access the Dashboard

- Check your internet connection.

- Ensure you're using a supported browser (Chrome, Firefox, Safari, Edge).

- Clear browser cache and cookies if the page isn't loading.

Meeting Not Showing Up in the Dashboard

- Confirm you are logged into the correct Zoom account.

- Check filters—ensure you're viewing "Upcoming" or "Past" meetings correctly.

Missing Recordings in the Dashboard

- If a cloud recording is missing, check your storage limits.

- If a local recording is missing, check the default save location on your computer.

Conclusion

Mastering the Zoom Dashboard is essential for efficiently managing your meetings, recordings, and settings. By familiarizing yourself with its key features—such as scheduling meetings, accessing recordings, adjusting settings, and troubleshooting common issues—you can maximize your Zoom experience.

Now that you have a complete understanding of the Zoom Dashboard, the next step is learning how to host and join meetings, which we will cover in the next chapter.

1.2.3 Understanding User Roles and Permissions

When using Zoom, understanding user roles and permissions is essential for managing meetings effectively and ensuring a secure and organized virtual environment. Zoom provides different user roles, each with distinct permissions and responsibilities. Whether you are an individual user, a business professional, or an IT administrator managing an organization's Zoom account, knowing these roles will help you control access, delegate responsibilities, and optimize your Zoom experience.

1. Understanding Zoom User Roles

Zoom offers several predefined user roles, each with varying levels of permissions. These roles help ensure proper management of meetings, webinars, and administrative functions within an organization.

Basic User Roles in Zoom

At a fundamental level, Zoom users fall into one of the following categories:

1. **Owner** – The highest-level account administrator with full control over all settings and users.

2. **Administrator** – A user with access to manage settings and users but with limited control compared to the owner.

3. **Member** – A regular user who can schedule and host meetings but does not have administrative privileges.

4. **Guest** – A participant who joins meetings but does not have an account within the organization.

Each of these roles determines what a user can or cannot do within the Zoom platform, particularly in an organizational setting.

Detailed Breakdown of Zoom Roles and Their Permissions

Zoom roles are primarily designed for organizations using Zoom Business, Enterprise, and Education plans. These roles help distribute management tasks while maintaining control over the platform.

1.1 Owner Role

The **Owner** is the highest authority in a Zoom account. This role is automatically assigned to the person who creates the Zoom account. Owners have exclusive privileges that cannot be transferred unless reassigned.

Key Permissions:

- Assign or remove administrator privileges.

- Manage billing, subscriptions, and account settings.

- Control security policies, including single sign-on (SSO).

- Modify advanced Zoom features such as cloud recording retention.

- Delete the account or transfer ownership.

The Owner has the power to configure the entire Zoom environment and manage users across the organization.

1.2 Administrator Role

Administrators (Admins) assist the Owner in managing the account and can configure settings for the organization. This role is crucial for businesses with multiple departments or teams using Zoom.

Key Permissions:

- Add, remove, or modify users within the account.

- Manage account settings and meeting policies.

- Enable or disable features such as recording, screen sharing, and chat.

- Monitor meetings and control security settings.

- Access reporting and analytics for Zoom usage.

Admins act as intermediaries between the Owner and regular users, ensuring that meetings run smoothly and securely.

1.3 Member Role

Members are standard Zoom users who can host, join, and schedule meetings but have limited administrative access.

Key Permissions:

- Host and schedule Zoom meetings.

- Access meeting controls such as screen sharing, breakout rooms, and chat.

- Record meetings (if enabled by the administrator).

- Manage personal settings but not global account settings.

Members primarily use Zoom for day-to-day communication and collaboration without administrative responsibilities.

1.4 Guest Role

Guests are external participants who join meetings without being part of the organization's Zoom account.

Key Permissions:

- Join meetings with a link or Meeting ID.

- Use basic features such as chat, reactions, and screen viewing.

- Limited control over in-meeting settings (cannot host or manage participants).

Guests are commonly clients, partners, or individuals who need temporary access to a meeting.

2. Managing User Roles and Permissions

For organizations, managing user roles effectively is crucial to maintaining security and operational efficiency. Zoom provides an Admin Portal where Owners and Admins can assign roles, modify permissions, and monitor user activity.

Assigning Roles in Zoom

To assign roles to users in a Zoom Business or Enterprise account:

1. Log into the Zoom Web Portal as an Owner or Administrator.

2. Navigate to Admin → User Management → Roles.

3. Click Create a Role or Edit an Existing Role.

4. Select the desired permissions for the role.

5. Assign users to the role and save changes.

This process ensures that each user has the appropriate level of access for their responsibilities.

Customizing Permissions

In addition to predefined roles, Zoom allows administrators to customize permissions for specific tasks. For example:

- Restricting who can record meetings.

- Enabling or disabling private chat for specific users.

- Controlling who can share screens or use breakout rooms.

Custom roles allow greater flexibility in managing Zoom accounts according to the organization's needs.

3. Security Implications of User Roles and Permissions

User roles play a crucial role in maintaining **security and privacy** within Zoom meetings. Mismanaged roles can lead to unauthorized access, disruptions, and potential data breaches.

Preventing Unauthorized Access

To minimize security risks, administrators should:

- Limit administrative access to only necessary users.

- Enable two-factor authentication (2FA) for added security.

- Use waiting rooms and passcodes to control meeting access.

Avoiding Zoombombing

Zoombombing occurs when unauthorized individuals disrupt meetings. Proper role management can prevent this by:

- Restricting screen sharing to hosts only.

- Disabling "Join Before Host" to prevent unauthorized early access.

- Using authentication settings to allow only verified users to join meetings.

Managing Data and Recordings

Zoom recordings contain sensitive information, so access should be restricted. Admins can:

- Limit who can record meetings.

- Set automatic cloud recording retention policies.

- Restrict sharing of recorded content outside the organization.

By managing permissions properly, organizations can ensure compliance with data protection laws such as GDPR and HIPAA.

4. Best Practices for Managing Zoom Roles and Permissions

Here are some best practices for effectively managing user roles in Zoom:

1. Regularly review user roles – Ensure only necessary users have administrative access.

2. Enable security features – Use authentication, waiting rooms, and role-based access control.

3. Train users – Educate employees about their Zoom roles and security best practices.

4. Monitor Zoom activity – Use Zoom's reporting tools to track meetings and participant actions.

5. Limit guest access – Only allow external users when absolutely necessary.

Conclusion

Understanding and managing user roles and permissions in Zoom is crucial for maintaining security, efficiency, and organization within virtual meetings. Whether you are an individual user or part of a business, knowing the different roles—Owner, Admin, Member, and Guest—can help you use Zoom more effectively.

By carefully assigning roles, customizing permissions, and implementing security best practices, you can ensure a smooth, productive, and secure Zoom experience for all participants.

1.3 Installing Zoom on Different Devices

1.3.1 Installing Zoom on Windows and Mac

Introduction

Zoom has become one of the most widely used video conferencing tools, offering a seamless virtual communication experience. Whether you are using a Windows PC or a Mac, installing Zoom is a straightforward process that allows you to host or join meetings efficiently. In this section, we will provide a step-by-step guide to downloading, installing, and setting up Zoom on both Windows and Mac computers.

1. Preparing for Installation

Before installing Zoom, ensure that your computer meets the system requirements and has a stable internet connection.

System Requirements

For Windows:

- Operating System: Windows 7 or later

- Processor: Dual-core 2 GHz or higher

- RAM: At least 4 GB

- Internet Connection: Minimum 1.5 Mbps up/down for video calling

- Webcam and Microphone: Built-in or external for video and audio calls

For Mac:

- Operating System: macOS X 10.9 (Mavericks) or later

- Processor: Intel or Apple Silicon (M1/M2) processor

- RAM: At least 4 GB

- Internet Connection: Minimum 1.5 Mbps up/down for video calling

- Webcam and Microphone: Built-in or external for video and audio calls

Ensuring your device meets these requirements will help Zoom function smoothly and provide a better video conferencing experience.

---

2. Downloading Zoom on Windows

Accessing the Zoom Website

To download Zoom on Windows, follow these steps:

1. Open your web browser (Google Chrome, Microsoft Edge, or Mozilla Firefox).
2. Go to the official Zoom download page: https://zoom.us/download.
3. Under the **"Zoom Client for Meetings"** section, click the **"Download"** button.
4. The Zoom installer (ZoomInstaller.exe) will begin downloading. You can check the download progress in your browser's download bar.

Installing Zoom on Windows

Once the download is complete, follow these steps to install Zoom:

1. Locate the **ZoomInstaller.exe** file in your **Downloads** folder.
2. Double-click the file to start the installation process.
3. If prompted by **User Account Control (UAC)**, click **"Yes"** to allow Zoom to make changes to your device.
4. The installation process will start automatically. Wait for Zoom to install on your computer.
5. Once installed, Zoom will open automatically. You can also find the Zoom shortcut on your desktop or in the Start Menu.

Logging in to Zoom on Windows

After installation, you need to log in or sign up for a Zoom account.

1. Open the Zoom application.
2. Click **"Sign In"** if you already have an account.

3. If you don't have an account, click **"Sign Up Free"**, and follow the instructions to create a new account.

4. You can also sign in using **Google, Facebook, or SSO (Single Sign-On).**

3. Downloading Zoom on Mac

Accessing the Zoom Website

Downloading Zoom on Mac follows a similar process:

1. Open **Safari** or another web browser (Chrome, Firefox).

2. Go to https://zoom.us/download.

3. Under **"Zoom Client for Meetings"**, click **"Download"**.

4. The **Zoom.pkg** file will begin downloading.

Installing Zoom on Mac

Once the download is complete, follow these steps:

1. Locate the **Zoom.pkg** file in the **Downloads** folder.

2. Double-click the file to start the installation process.

3. The **Zoom Installer** window will appear. Click **"Continue"**.

4. Follow the on-screen instructions and click **"Install"** when prompted.

5. If asked, enter your **Mac administrator password** to proceed.

6. The installation will complete, and Zoom will be available in your **Applications** folder.

Granting Permissions for Zoom on Mac

Mac users may need to grant Zoom additional permissions for a seamless experience.

1. Go to **System Settings** (or System Preferences on older macOS versions).

2. Click **Privacy & Security**.

3. Under **Microphone**, check **Zoom** to allow audio access.

4. Under **Camera**, check **Zoom** to enable video access.

5. Under **Screen Recording**, enable **Zoom** if you plan to share your screen during meetings.

Without these permissions, Zoom may not function correctly for audio, video, or screen sharing.

4. Updating Zoom

Keeping Zoom up to date ensures you have the latest features and security patches.

Updating Zoom on Windows

1. Open the Zoom application.

2. Click on your **profile icon** in the top-right corner.

3. Select **"Check for Updates"**.

4. If an update is available, click **"Update"**, and Zoom will install the latest version.

Updating Zoom on Mac

1. Open the Zoom application.

2. Click **Zoom.us** in the top menu bar.

3. Select **"Check for Updates"**.

4. Click **"Update"** if a new version is available.

5. Troubleshooting Installation Issues

If you encounter issues while installing Zoom, here are some troubleshooting tips:

Common Windows Installation Issues

• Zoom Installer won't open: Try running the installer as an administrator by right-clicking and selecting "Run as Administrator."

• Installation stuck or taking too long: Check your internet connection and temporarily disable antivirus software.

- Error messages during installation: Restart your computer and try reinstalling.

Common Mac Installation Issues

- Mac won't open the Zoom.pkg file: Go to System Settings > Privacy & Security and allow apps downloaded from "App Store and identified developers."

- Permissions not granted: Revisit System Settings > Privacy & Security to manually enable permissions.

6. Uninstalling Zoom (If Needed)

If you ever need to uninstall Zoom, follow these steps:

Uninstalling Zoom on Windows

1. Open the **Control Panel** and go to **Programs > Uninstall a program**.

2. Find **Zoom** in the list and click **Uninstall**.

3. Follow the prompts to remove Zoom completely.

Uninstalling Zoom on Mac

1. Open **Finder** and go to **Applications**.

2. Find **Zoom.us** and drag it to the **Trash**.

3. Empty the Trash to remove Zoom completely.

7. Conclusion

Installing Zoom on Windows and Mac is a simple process that takes just a few minutes. By following this guide, you can successfully download, install, and set up Zoom for a smooth video conferencing experience. Once installed, you can explore various features, join meetings, and enhance your virtual communication.

1.3.2 Using Zoom on Mobile (iOS and Android)

Zoom is widely used across different devices, including mobile phones and tablets. Whether you're using an iPhone, iPad, or Android device, Zoom's mobile app provides a convenient way to attend, host, and manage meetings on the go. This section will guide you through downloading, setting up, and using Zoom on mobile devices, ensuring a seamless experience for virtual meetings.

Downloading and Installing Zoom on Mobile

Before you can start using Zoom on your iOS or Android device, you need to download and install the Zoom app. Here's how to do it:

For iOS (iPhone/iPad)

1. Open the App Store: On your iPhone or iPad, tap the App Store icon.

2. Search for Zoom: In the search bar, type "Zoom Cloud Meetings" and look for the official Zoom app.

3. Download the App: Tap the Download (cloud) icon or Get button to start downloading.

4. Install and Open: Once installed, tap Open to launch the Zoom app.

For Android Devices

1. Open Google Play Store: On your Android device, open the Google Play Store.

2. Search for Zoom: Type "Zoom Cloud Meetings" in the search bar.

3. Install the App: Tap Install, and wait for the installation to complete.

4. Open Zoom: Once installed, tap Open to launch the app.

Important Notes:

- Ensure your device meets the system requirements for the Zoom app.

- Keep your Zoom app updated to access the latest features and security updates.

- You can also download the Zoom app from Zoom's official website if needed.

Signing In and Navigating the Mobile Interface

Once you've installed the Zoom app, you need to sign in or create an account.

Signing In to Zoom

1. Open the Zoom app on your mobile device.

2. Tap "Sign In" if you already have a Zoom account.

3. Enter your email and password, then tap Sign In.

4. You can also sign in using Google, Apple, Facebook, or SSO (Single Sign-On).

5. If you don't have an account, tap "Sign Up" and follow the registration steps.

Navigating the Zoom Mobile Interface

Once signed in, you'll see the main dashboard with these options:

- Meet & Chat – Quick access to start or join meetings.

- Meetings – View and manage scheduled meetings.

- Contacts – See your saved contacts and invite new ones.

- Settings – Adjust audio, video, security, and account settings.

The interface is user-friendly, but familiarizing yourself with each section will make using Zoom more efficient.

Joining a Meeting on Mobile

Joining a Zoom meeting on mobile is easy and can be done in multiple ways.

Method 1: Using a Meeting Link

- If you receive a meeting invitation via email, WhatsApp, or any other app, simply tap the meeting link to open Zoom and join the session.

Method 2: Entering a Meeting ID

1. Open the Zoom app.

2. Tap Join on the home screen.

3. Enter the Meeting ID provided by the host.

4. Input the Meeting Passcode if required.

5. Choose whether to enable or disable audio and video before joining.

6. Tap Join Meeting.

Method 3: Joining from the Zoom Calendar

- If your meeting is scheduled in Zoom, go to the Meetings tab and tap Join for the upcoming session.

Hosting a Zoom Meeting on Mobile

If you are the host, you can start a meeting directly from your phone.

Starting an Instant Meeting

1. Open the Zoom app and tap New Meeting.

2. Choose whether to start with video on/off.

3. Tap Start Meeting to begin the session.

4. Tap Participants to invite others via email, contacts, or a meeting link.

Scheduling a Meeting

1. Tap Schedule on the Zoom app.

2. Enter the meeting details:

   o Meeting Name

   o Date and Time

   o Meeting ID & Passcode

   o Waiting Room and Security Settings

3. Tap Save, and Zoom will add the meeting to your calendar if linked.

Managing Audio and Video on Mobile

Enabling and Muting Audio

- Tap the Microphone icon to mute/unmute.

- Tap Join Audio and select Call via Device Audio for better sound quality.

- Use a headset or external microphone for clearer sound.

Turning Video On/Off

- Tap the Camera icon to enable/disable video.

- Go to Settings > Video to adjust video quality.

- Use Virtual Backgrounds (on compatible devices) for a professional look.

Using Screen Sharing on Mobile

1. Tap Share Content during a meeting.

2. Select what to share:

   o Screen (Full mobile screen sharing)

   o Photos or Files

   o Whiteboard

   o Website URL

3. Tap Start Now, and participants will see your shared content.

4. Tap Stop Sharing when done.

Chat, Reactions, and Breakout Rooms on Mobile

Using the Chat Feature

- Tap Chat to send messages to participants.

- Send private or group messages.

- Share files, links, and emojis.

Using Reactions and Polls

- Tap Reactions to use emojis like 👍, 👏, or raise hand ✋.

- Participate in polls if enabled by the host.

Breakout Rooms on Mobile

- If the host assigns you to a Breakout Room, you'll receive a notification to join.

- Tap Join Breakout Room to move into a smaller session.

- You can return to the main meeting anytime.

Security and Privacy on Zoom Mobile

To ensure a secure meeting experience:

- Use Passcodes & Waiting Rooms for security.

- Lock Meetings once all participants have joined.

- Enable End-to-End Encryption in settings.

- Remove unwanted participants using the Manage Participants feature.

Troubleshooting Common Zoom Issues on Mobile

Here are **some common issues and solutions**:

1. App Crashes or Freezes

- Ensure Zoom is updated.

- Restart your phone or tablet.

- Clear app cache (Android only).

2. Audio or Microphone Issues

- Check device permissions for microphone access.

- Test audio in Zoom settings.

- Switch to headphones for better sound quality.

3. Poor Video Quality or Connection Drops

- Use a strong Wi-Fi connection.

- Close other apps running in the background.

- Lower video resolution if bandwidth is low.

Conclusion

Using Zoom on mobile devices provides great flexibility for virtual meetings, webinars, and team collaborations. By following the steps in this guide, you can join, host, and manage meetings efficiently, no matter where you are.

1.3.3 Zoom Web Client vs. Zoom Desktop App

Zoom offers multiple ways to access and use its platform, with the **Zoom Web Client** and the **Zoom Desktop App** being the two most commonly used options. Each version has its own strengths, limitations, and ideal use cases. In this section, we will explore the differences between the Zoom Web Client and the Zoom Desktop App, helping you understand which option is best suited for your needs.

1. Understanding the Zoom Web Client

1.1 What is the Zoom Web Client?

The Zoom Web Client is a browser-based version of Zoom that allows users to join and host meetings without installing any additional software. It provides a convenient way to use Zoom when downloading the desktop application is not an option.

The Web Client runs on most modern browsers, including Google Chrome, Mozilla Firefox, Microsoft Edge, and Safari. However, some features may be restricted depending on the browser used.

1.2 How to Access the Zoom Web Client

To access Zoom via a web browser, follow these steps:

1. Open your preferred browser.

2. Go to https://zoom.us.

3. Click on **"Join a Meeting"** (if joining) or **"Sign In"** to start or schedule a meeting.

Join Meeting

Meeting ID or Personal Link Name

Enter Meeting ID or Personal Link Name

Join

Join a meeting from an H.323/SIP room system

4. Enter the **Meeting ID** or **Personal Meeting Link** provided by the host.

5. When prompted, click **"Join from Your Browser"** instead of downloading the desktop app.

6. Allow microphone and camera permissions to participate in the meeting.

Note: In some cases, you may need to log into your Zoom account before joining a meeting from a browser.

1.3 Features of the Zoom Web Client

The Zoom Web Client provides essential features for participating in meetings:

- Joining and hosting meetings

- Using chat and reactions

- Screen sharing (limited browser support)

- Viewing shared screens

- Managing participants (for hosts and co-hosts)

- Basic audio and video controls

However, certain features are **restricted or unavailable**, depending on the browser used. For example, some browsers may not support virtual backgrounds, advanced screen sharing, or high-quality audio processing.

1.4 Limitations of the Zoom Web Client

Despite its convenience, the Zoom Web Client has several limitations:

- Reduced performance: Web-based applications tend to consume more browser memory, potentially causing lag.

- Limited audio/video settings: Users have fewer customization options compared to the desktop app.

- No virtual backgrounds: Many browsers do not support Zoom's virtual background feature.

- Restricted recording options: You cannot record meetings to your local device via the web client.

- Limited gallery view: The web client does not support the full grid view of all participants.

2. Understanding the Zoom Desktop App

2.1 What is the Zoom Desktop App?

The Zoom Desktop App is a standalone application that provides the full suite of Zoom features. Unlike the Web Client, it offers a smoother experience, higher quality audio and video, and a wider range of functionalities.

2.2 How to Download and Install the Zoom Desktop App

To install the Zoom Desktop App:

1. Visit https://zoom.us/download.

2. Under **"Zoom Desktop Client"**, click **"Download"**.

3. Once downloaded, open the installation file and follow the on-screen instructions.

4. Launch Zoom and sign in to your account.

Tip: Keeping your Zoom Desktop App updated ensures access to the latest features and security improvements.

2.3 Features of the Zoom Desktop App

The Zoom Desktop App provides an extensive set of features, including:

- Full-screen and gallery views
- Customizable video settings, including virtual backgrounds
- Advanced screen sharing with multiple options
- Meeting recording (local and cloud storage options)
- Integration with third-party apps and plugins
- Breakout rooms for group discussions
- More stable audio and video performance

2.4 Advantages of the Zoom Desktop App

Compared to the Web Client, the Zoom Desktop App offers significant benefits:

✓ Better video and audio quality – Uses system resources efficiently to deliver higher resolution and smoother performance.

✓ More control for hosts and co-hosts – Easier management of participants, breakout rooms, and meeting settings.

✓ Greater compatibility with integrations – Works seamlessly with apps like Outlook, Slack, Google Calendar, and more.

✓ Full access to recording features – Allows local and cloud recordings, unlike the Web Client.

2.5 Limitations of the Zoom Desktop App

Although the Zoom Desktop App is the preferred method for most users, it does have some downsides:

- Requires installation – Some corporate or school devices may have restrictions on installing software.

- Consumes storage space – Unlike the Web Client, which runs in a browser, the desktop app takes up space on your computer.

- Frequent updates – Users need to keep the app updated to access new features and security patches.

3. Key Differences: Zoom Web Client vs. Zoom Desktop App

Feature	Zoom Web Client	Zoom Desktop App
Installation Required?	No	Yes
Meeting Quality	Moderate (depends on browser)	High (optimized performance)
Audio & Video Settings	Limited	Full control
Screen Sharing	Available but limited	Full functionality
Recording Options	Cloud recording only (if enabled by host)	Local & cloud recording
Virtual Backgrounds	Not supported	Fully supported
Breakout Rooms	Can join but cannot manage	Full control (create & manage)
Performance	Can be laggy in browsers	Smooth and stable experience

4. Which One Should You Use?

Choose the Zoom Web Client if:

✔ You cannot install software (e.g., using a shared or work computer).

✔ You need a quick way to join a meeting without downloading Zoom.

✔ You are only attending a meeting and do not need advanced features.

Choose the Zoom Desktop App if:

✓ You host meetings regularly and need full control over settings.

✓ You require high-quality video, audio, and recording features.

✓ You need access to advanced features like Breakout Rooms and virtual backgrounds.

Pro Tip: If you frequently use Zoom for work, education, or personal meetings, installing the **Zoom Desktop App** is highly recommended.

---

5. Conclusion

Both the Zoom Web Client and the Zoom Desktop App provide access to Zoom's powerful video conferencing features, but they serve different purposes. The Web Client is a lightweight, browser-based option for quick access, while the Desktop App provides a full-featured, high-performance experience.

For occasional users or those with restrictions on downloading software, the Web Client is a suitable alternative. However, for anyone looking to leverage the full potential of Zoom, the Desktop App remains the best choice.

By understanding the differences between these two options, you can select the version that best fits your needs and optimize your Zoom experience accordingly.

CHAPTER II
Hosting and Joining Meetings

2.1 Scheduling a Zoom Meeting

2.1.1 How to Schedule a Meeting

Scheduling a Zoom meeting is an essential skill for anyone looking to host virtual gatherings, whether for business meetings, online classes, social events, or webinars. This section provides a comprehensive, step-by-step guide on how to schedule a meeting in Zoom, covering all the necessary settings and customization options to ensure a seamless experience.

Understanding Zoom Meeting Scheduling

Before diving into the step-by-step instructions, it's essential to understand why scheduling a meeting instead of using the "Instant Meeting" option is beneficial:

- **Advanced Preparation**: Scheduling allows you to set up everything in advance, ensuring participants receive invitations ahead of time.

- **Consistency**: If you're hosting recurring meetings, scheduling eliminates the need to generate a new link each time.

- **Customization**: You can configure settings such as passwords, waiting rooms, and participant permissions before the meeting begins.

Step-by-Step Guide to Scheduling a Zoom Meeting

1. Scheduling a Meeting on the Zoom Desktop App (Windows & Mac)

1. **Open Zoom**:

   o Launch the **Zoom Desktop Client** on your computer.

   o Sign in to your Zoom account if you haven't already.

2. **Go to the "Schedule" Option**:

   o Click on the **"Schedule"** button (calendar icon) located on the home screen of the Zoom app.

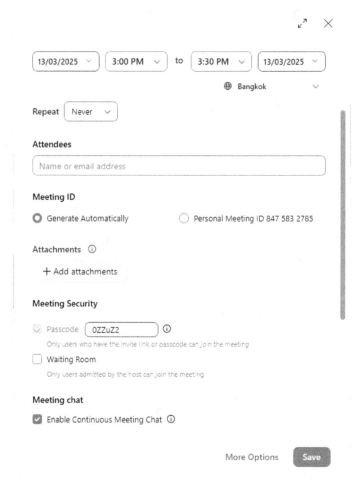

3. **Enter Meeting Details**:

   o **Topic**: Type a title for your meeting (e.g., "Weekly Team Sync" or "Client Presentation").

   o **Description (Optional)**: Add additional details about the meeting.

4. **Set the Date and Time**:

   o Choose the date and time for the meeting.

   o Select the duration (this is for reference only; the meeting won't automatically end).

   o Adjust the time zone if needed.

5. **Configure Meeting ID and Security Settings**:

   o Meeting ID: Choose between:

      ▪ Generate Automatically: Zoom creates a unique meeting ID.

      ▪ Personal Meeting ID (PMI): Use a fixed meeting ID (best for internal recurring meetings).

   o Security Options:

      ▪ Passcode: Set a password to restrict unauthorized access.

      ▪ Waiting Room: Enable this if you want to manually admit participants.

6. **Video and Audio Settings**:

   o Host Video: Choose whether the host's video is on/off by default.

   o Participant Video: Choose whether participants' video is on/off when they join.

   o Audio Options:

      ▪ Telephone & Computer Audio: Allows participants to join using phone or device audio.

      ▪ Only Computer Audio: Limits participants to using their device's microphone.

7. **Advanced Meeting Options**:

   o Enable Join Before Host: Allows participants to enter the meeting before the host starts it.

   o Mute Participants Upon Entry: Useful for large meetings to reduce background noise.

   o Automatically Record Meeting: Choose to record the meeting either locally or on the cloud.

8. **Calendar Integration (Optional)**:

   o Choose to add the scheduled meeting to Google Calendar, Outlook, or Other Calendars.

9. **Save and Send Invitations**:

   o Click "Schedule" to finalize.

   o Copy the invitation details or use the calendar integration to send invites.

---

2. Scheduling a Meeting on the Zoom Web Portal

1. **Go to Zoom's Website**:

   o Open your web browser and visit zoom.us.

   o Log in to your account.

2. **Access the Meeting Scheduler**:

   o Click on **"Schedule a Meeting"** at the top right corner.

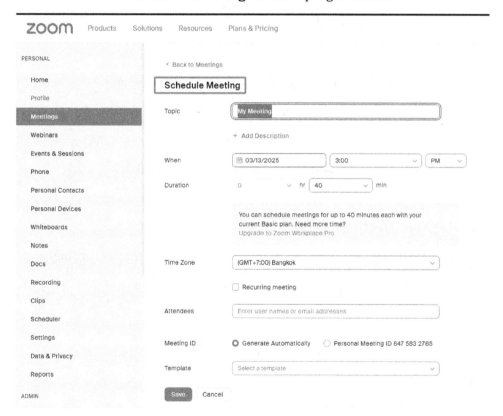

3. **Fill in Meeting Details** (similar to the desktop app):

   - Title, Description, Date, Time, and Time Zone.

   - Meeting ID and Security Settings.

   - Video, Audio, and Advanced Options.

4. **Calendar Integration and Invite Options**:

   - Select the calendar type for sending invitations (Google, Outlook, or others).

5. **Save and Copy Invitation Link**:

   - Once scheduled, copy the invitation details to share with participants.

3. Scheduling a Meeting on the Zoom Mobile App (iOS & Android)

1. Open the Zoom App and Sign In.

2. Tap on "Schedule" (calendar icon).

3. Enter Meeting Information (Topic, Date, Time, Security, and Video settings).

4. Set Advanced Options (Waiting Room, Recording, and Audio Preferences).

5. Choose a Calendar Integration and Save.

6. Send Invitations via Calendar or Copy the Meeting Link.

Customizing Your Meeting for Specific Needs

Depending on your meeting type, you may want to tweak settings accordingly:

1. Business Meetings

- Use **waiting rooms** to control access.

- Mute participants upon entry to avoid distractions.

- Enable **recording** for reference.

2. Webinars and Large Events

- Use **registration** for tracking attendees.

- Assign **co-hosts** or **panelists** for better management.

- Disable participant screen sharing for security.

3. Online Classes and Training Sessions

- Use **breakout rooms** for group activities.

- Enable **polls and Q&A** for engagement.

- Record sessions for students who missed the class.

Common Issues and Troubleshooting

1. Meeting Not Appearing in Calendar

- Ensure you selected the correct calendar during scheduling.

- Manually add the meeting using the invitation link.

2. Time Zone Mismatch

- Double-check the time zone settings in both Zoom and your calendar.

3. Participants Not Receiving Invitations

- Resend invites manually via email or messaging apps.

- Verify email settings to ensure messages aren't in spam folders.

4. Meeting Link Not Working

- Regenerate and resend the link if necessary.

- Confirm meeting settings allow participants to join.

Conclusion

Scheduling a Zoom meeting is a straightforward process, yet it offers a range of advanced features that can enhance your virtual interactions. By understanding how to properly configure settings, integrate with calendars, and troubleshoot common issues, you can ensure your meetings run smoothly and efficiently. Whether you're hosting a business meeting, an online class, or a social gathering, mastering Zoom's scheduling tools will improve your virtual communication experience.

2.1.2 Setting Up Recurring Meetings

Introduction to Recurring Meetings in Zoom

Recurring meetings in Zoom allow users to schedule a series of meetings that take place at regular intervals. Instead of manually scheduling a new meeting each time, users can create a recurring meeting with the same link, settings, and participants. This feature is particularly useful for team check-ins, online classes, training sessions, and any event that occurs on a consistent schedule.

This section will guide you through the steps to set up recurring meetings, explore different recurrence options, and understand how to manage these meetings effectively.

Why Use Recurring Meetings?

Recurring meetings save time and ensure consistency in scheduling. Some benefits include:

- **Convenience:** Participants use the same meeting link each time, avoiding confusion.

- **Time-Saving:** You don't have to set up a new meeting repeatedly.

- **Consistency:** Helps in maintaining a structured schedule, especially for businesses and educational institutions.

- **Automated Reminders:** Integrated calendar options can send automatic reminders.

Step-by-Step Guide to Setting Up Recurring Meetings

Step 1: Open Zoom and Navigate to Scheduling

1. Sign in to your Zoom account via the desktop app, web portal, or mobile app.

2. Click on **"Schedule a Meeting"** at the top-right corner of the screen.

3. Enter the meeting **title, description, and time** as required.

Step 2: Enable Recurrence

1. Find the **"Recurrence"** option under the date and time settings.

2. Select **"Recurring meeting"** to unlock additional options.

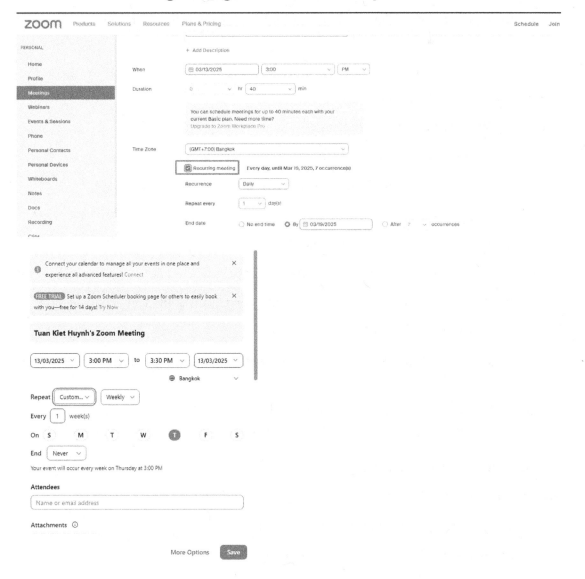

Step 3: Choose the Recurrence Frequency

Zoom provides multiple recurrence options to suit different scheduling needs:

- **Daily:** The meeting occurs every day at the same time.

- **Weekly:** Ideal for weekly team meetings, classes, or events.

- **Monthly:** Perfect for monthly check-ins or progress reviews.

- **No Fixed Time:** If the schedule varies but the same link is needed, this option allows flexibility.

Configuring Recurring Meeting Options

Setting Up Weekly Recurring Meetings

- Select **"Weekly"** under recurrence settings.

- Choose the **specific days of the week** (e.g., Monday and Wednesday).

- Set an **end date** or define the number of occurrences (e.g., repeat for 12 weeks).

Setting Up Monthly Recurring Meetings

- Choose **"Monthly"** and select the **specific date** (e.g., the 15th of each month).

- If preferred, select **"The first Monday of every month"** instead of a fixed date.

Using "No Fixed Time" Option

- This setting allows you to **reuse the meeting link** without scheduling specific times.

- Best for informal or flexible meetings where timing varies.

Managing and Editing Recurring Meetings

Editing a Recurring Meeting

If a recurring meeting's schedule changes, you can edit it by:

1. Navigating to **"Meetings"** in the Zoom app or web portal.

2. Clicking on the specific recurring meeting.

3. Selecting **"Edit"** to modify the schedule, duration, or settings.

4. Choosing **"Edit This Occurrence"** or **"Edit All Occurrences"** (if applying changes to all sessions).

Cancelling a Recurring Meeting

To delete or cancel a recurring meeting:

- Go to the **Meetings** tab in Zoom.

- Select the recurring meeting.

- Click **"Delete"** and choose whether to remove a single occurrence or all future occurrences.

Advanced Features for Recurring Meetings

Using Personal Meeting ID (PMI) for Recurring Meetings

Instead of generating a new meeting ID, you can:

- Enable Personal Meeting ID (PMI) for a consistent link.

- Use PMI for one-on-one check-ins or small team meetings.

- Ensure privacy by requiring a password or waiting room.

Enabling Automatic Recording for Recurring Meetings

For training sessions or lectures, enable "Automatically record meeting":

- Go to Meeting Options when scheduling.

- Select "Record automatically on the local computer" or "Record in the cloud".

Setting Up Alternative Hosts and Co-Hosts

- Assign alternative hosts to manage recurring meetings when the primary host is unavailable.

- Use co-hosts to help facilitate discussions and manage participants.

Best Practices for Recurring Meetings

1. Use a Consistent Meeting Link – Avoid confusion by using the same link for all sessions.

2. Test Settings Beforehand – Ensure correct permissions and security settings.

3. Enable Reminders – Use calendar integrations to remind participants.

4. Monitor Engagement – Utilize Zoom analytics to track attendance.

5. Ensure Security – Enable passcodes, waiting rooms, and disable screen sharing for unauthorized users.

Conclusion

Recurring meetings in Zoom streamline scheduling and enhance efficiency for organizations, educators, and businesses. By properly setting up and managing recurring meetings, you can ensure smooth, organized, and professional virtual interactions.

2.1.3 Time Zone and Calendar Integration

Introduction

Scheduling meetings across different time zones can be challenging, especially when working with international teams or clients. Zoom provides built-in tools to help users set up meetings with accurate time zone configurations, minimizing confusion and ensuring that all participants join at the right time. Additionally, Zoom integrates seamlessly with popular calendar applications like Google Calendar, Microsoft Outlook, and Apple Calendar, making it easier to schedule, track, and manage meetings.

In this section, we will explore how to set the correct time zone in Zoom, use calendar integrations, and ensure that participants across different regions receive accurate meeting details.

1. Understanding Time Zones in Zoom

1.1 Why Time Zones Matter in Scheduling

When scheduling a Zoom meeting, the time zone setting determines when invitations are sent and when the meeting will take place. If a meeting is scheduled without adjusting the time zone correctly, participants in different locations may receive incorrect timings, leading to missed or delayed meetings.

Time zone considerations are especially important for:

- Remote teams with employees across different regions.

- Client meetings where participants are located in various parts of the world.

- Webinars and virtual events involving a global audience.

- Educational sessions with international students.

1.2 Setting the Correct Time Zone in Zoom

To ensure accurate scheduling, follow these steps to set your time zone in Zoom:

Changing the Time Zone in Your Zoom Account

1. Log into your Zoom account at zoom.us.

2. Click on your profile picture in the top-right corner and select Settings.

3. Under the Profile section, locate the Time Zone option.

4. Click Edit and choose your correct time zone from the drop-down menu.

5. Click Save to apply the changes.

Setting the Time Zone When Scheduling a Meeting

When scheduling a new meeting, Zoom allows you to specify a different time zone than your default setting:

1. Go to **Meetings** in your Zoom dashboard.

2. Click **Schedule a Meeting**.

3. In the **Time Zone** section, click the drop-down menu and select the appropriate time zone.

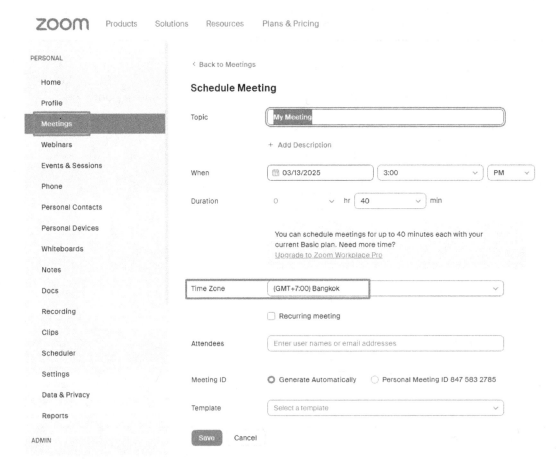

4. Proceed with scheduling and invite attendees as needed.

This feature is useful when organizing meetings for participants in different regions while keeping your personal settings unchanged.

2. Integrating Zoom with Calendar Applications

2.1 Benefits of Calendar Integration

Connecting Zoom with a calendar application offers several advantages:

- Automatic synchronization: Scheduled Zoom meetings appear in your calendar automatically.

- Easy meeting reminders: Receive notifications about upcoming meetings.

- Seamless invitation process: Automatically send meeting invites with Zoom details.

- One-click meeting join links: Participants can join directly from the calendar.

2.2 How to Integrate Zoom with Google Calendar

Google Calendar is one of the most widely used scheduling tools. To connect Zoom with Google Calendar:

Connecting Zoom to Google Calendar

1. Log into your **Zoom account** and go to the **Zoom App Marketplace** (marketplace.zoom.us).

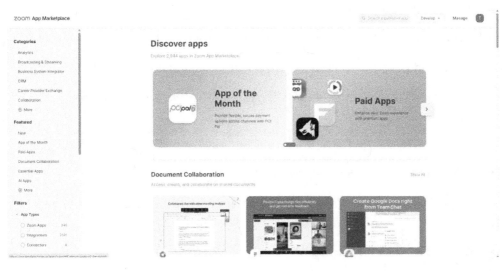

2. Search for **Google Calendar** and click **Add**.

3. Grant the necessary permissions to allow Zoom to access your calendar.

4. Once connected, Zoom meetings will automatically sync with Google Calendar.

Scheduling a Zoom Meeting via Google Calendar

1. Open **Google Calendar**.

2. Click **Create Event**.

3. Add the meeting title, date, and time.

4. Click **Add Video Conferencing** → Select **Zoom Meeting**.

5. Click **Save**, and the Zoom meeting details will be included in the invite.

This integration ensures that meeting details, including join links and passwords, are easily accessible to all attendees.

2.3 How to Integrate Zoom with Microsoft Outlook

For users who prefer Microsoft Outlook, Zoom offers an add-in that simplifies meeting scheduling:

Installing the Zoom Add-in for Outlook

1. Open **Microsoft Outlook** and go to the **Add-ins Store**.

2. Search for **Zoom for Outlook** and click **Add**.

3. Sign in with your Zoom account to link it with Outlook.

Scheduling a Zoom Meeting via Outlook

1. Open **Outlook Calendar**.

2. Click **New Event**.

3. In the toolbar, select **Add a Zoom Meeting**.

4. Configure meeting settings and invite participants.

5. Click **Save & Send Invitations**.

Now, your Zoom meetings will automatically appear in your Outlook calendar, making it easier to manage your schedule.

2.4 How to Integrate Zoom with Apple Calendar

Apple users can also integrate Zoom with iCloud Calendar for better meeting organization.

Enabling Zoom and Apple Calendar Sync

1. Open **Zoom Settings** on your Mac or iPhone.

2. Navigate to **Calendar Integration**.

3. Select **Apple Calendar** and allow permissions.

Scheduling a Zoom Meeting via Apple Calendar

1. Open **Apple Calendar**.

2. Click **New Event** and enter meeting details.

3. Copy and paste the **Zoom meeting link** into the location field.

4. Save the event and send invitations.

This ensures that all Apple users receive meeting reminders and easy access to Zoom meetings.

3. Troubleshooting Time Zone and Calendar Issues

Common Time Zone Issues and Fixes

- **Issue**: Participants receive incorrect meeting times.

    - **Solution**: Double-check the meeting time zone when scheduling.

- **Issue**: Zoom meetings appear at the wrong time in the calendar.

    - **Solution**: Ensure the calendar app and Zoom use the same time zone settings.

- **Issue**: Meetings do not sync with the calendar.

    - **Solution**: Reauthorize the calendar integration in Zoom settings.

Ensuring Accurate Calendar Sync

To avoid scheduling conflicts, follow these best practices:

- Keep your **calendar and Zoom time zones** consistent.

- Always enable **meeting reminders**.

- Regularly check for **Zoom updates** to ensure calendar integrations function properly.

Conclusion

Effective time zone management and calendar integration are essential for seamless Zoom meeting scheduling. By setting the correct time zone and integrating Zoom with Google Calendar, Microsoft Outlook, or Apple Calendar, you can ensure that participants receive accurate meeting details. With these tools, you can reduce scheduling confusion, improve meeting attendance, and enhance overall productivity.

By following the best practices outlined in this guide, you can confidently schedule Zoom meetings that accommodate participants across different regions while staying organized and efficient.

2.2 Joining a Zoom Meeting

2.2.1 Joining via Link or Meeting ID

Joining a Zoom meeting is a simple process, but understanding the different methods available can ensure a smooth and hassle-free experience. Whether you receive an invitation link via email or need to manually enter a Meeting ID, this section will guide you through the process step by step.

Understanding Zoom Meeting Invitations

Before joining a Zoom meeting, it is important to understand how meeting invitations work. Typically, the host of a Zoom meeting will send an invitation containing:

- A direct **meeting link** (URL) that allows participants to join with one click.

- A **Meeting ID**, a unique numerical code assigned to each meeting.

- A **passcode** (if required) for additional security.

Zoom invitations can be sent via email, chat applications, calendar events, or posted in online communities.

Method 1: Joining a Zoom Meeting via Link

Joining via a direct invitation link is the easiest and fastest way to enter a Zoom meeting. Here's how you can do it:

Step 1: Click the Invitation Link

- Open your email, messaging app, or calendar event where the invitation was shared.

- Click on the provided Zoom meeting link (e.g., https://zoom.us/j/123456789).

Step 2: Open the Zoom Application

- If Zoom is installed on your device, your browser may prompt you to **"Open Zoom Meetings"** or **"Launch Zoom"**. Click "Open" to proceed.

- If Zoom is not installed, you may be asked to **download and install Zoom** or **join from your web browser**.

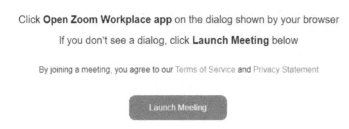

Step 3: Enter Your Name (If Required)

- If you are not logged in to a Zoom account, Zoom may prompt you to enter a display name before joining the meeting.

- This name will be visible to other participants.

Step 4: Adjust Audio and Video Settings

- Choose whether to **join with computer audio** or **phone audio** (if available).

- You can also decide whether to turn your **camera on or off** before entering the meeting.

Step 5: Wait for the Host to Admit You (If Necessary)

- If the meeting has a **Waiting Room enabled**, you will see a message stating, **"Please wait, the meeting host will let you in soon."**

- Once the host admits you, you will enter the meeting.

Step 6: Participate in the Meeting

- Once inside, you can use features like **chat, screen sharing, and reactions** to interact with others.

Troubleshooting Common Issues When Joining via Link

Issue	Solution
Link not working	Check if the link is correct and has not expired. Copy and paste it into your browser if clicking doesn't work.
Browser does not open Zoom	Manually launch the Zoom app and enter the Meeting ID.
Stuck on "Connecting" screen	Check your internet connection and try restarting Zoom.
Meeting is full	If the host has set a participant limit, you may not be able to join. Contact the host for assistance.

Method 2: Joining a Zoom Meeting via Meeting ID

If you do not have a direct link, you can join using a **Meeting ID**. This is useful when links are not accessible or when joining a meeting from a different device.

Step 1: Open the Zoom Application

- Launch Zoom on your **Windows, Mac, iOS, Android, or web browser**.

Step 2: Click "Join a Meeting"

- On the Zoom home screen, click the **"Join"** button.

Step 3: Enter the Meeting ID

- Type in the **9, 10, or 11-digit** Meeting ID provided by the host (e.g., 123-456-789).

Step 4: Enter the Meeting Passcode (If Required)

- If the host has set up a **passcode**, you will need to enter it to proceed.
- The passcode is usually included in the invitation.

Step 5: Adjust Your Display Name and Settings

- Enter your preferred **name** that will be displayed to other participants.
- Choose whether to **join with video on or off**.

Step 6: Join the Meeting

- Click **"Join"**, and you will enter the meeting or the waiting room (if enabled).

Joining from a Web Browser

If you do not have the Zoom app installed, you can join via browser:

- Open https://zoom.us/join in your web browser.
- Enter the **Meeting ID** and click **"Join"**.
- If a passcode is required, enter it when prompted.

Method 3: Joining via Phone (Dial-in Option)

For participants without internet access, Zoom provides a **dial-in** option to join via phone:

Step 1: Find the Dial-in Number

- The invitation will contain a list of phone numbers (e.g., +1 646 558 8656 US).

- Choose the number closest to your location.

Step 2: Dial the Number and Enter the Meeting ID

- Call the selected number and listen to the automated instructions.

- Enter the **Meeting ID** using your phone's keypad, followed by the # **key**.

Step 3: Enter the Participant ID (If Applicable)

- If prompted for a **participant ID**, press # to skip unless you have one.

Step 4: Join the Meeting

- You will now be connected to the meeting's **audio**.

- If you also join from a computer, mute one device to avoid audio feedback.

Common Issues When Dialing In

Issue	Solution
Can't connect to meeting audio	Ensure you dialed the correct number and entered the right Meeting ID.
Audio is muted	Some meetings have participant audio muted by default. Press *6 to unmute.
Poor call quality	Try dialing in from a different number or using an internet connection instead.

Best Practices for Joining a Zoom Meeting

To ensure a seamless experience when joining a Zoom meeting, keep the following tips in mind:

Before the Meeting:

✓ Check the meeting details – Ensure you have the correct link, Meeting ID, and passcode.

✓ Test your internet connection – A strong and stable connection prevents audio/video lag.

✓ Install Zoom updates – Always use the latest version for improved performance and security.

✓ Find a quiet environment – Avoid background noise for a better meeting experience.

During the Meeting:

✓ Mute yourself when not speaking – Reduces background noise and keeps the meeting professional.

✓ Turn on video when necessary – Helps with engagement and communication.

✓ Use chat and reactions – Non-verbal interactions can enhance participation.

Conclusion

Joining a Zoom meeting is simple, but choosing the right method depends on your situation. Whether you **click a link, enter a Meeting ID, or dial in by phone**, following the correct steps ensures a smooth experience. By understanding potential issues and best practices, you can confidently join any Zoom meeting with ease.

2.2.2 Troubleshooting Common Joining Issues

Joining a Zoom meeting should be a straightforward process, but users often encounter technical issues that prevent them from connecting smoothly. Whether it's due to connectivity problems, incorrect meeting credentials, or system compatibility issues, troubleshooting these problems efficiently can save time and frustration. This section will cover the most common joining issues, their causes, and step-by-step solutions to resolve them.

1. Connection Issues

One of the most frequent problems users face when joining a Zoom meeting is related to their internet connection. If your network is unstable or slow, Zoom may struggle to connect or experience delays.

Symptoms:

- Zoom takes too long to connect or does not connect at all.

- Audio and video lag or freeze intermittently.

- The "Unable to connect" error message appears.

Solutions:

1.1 Check Your Internet Connection

- Open a web browser and try loading a website to see if your internet is working.

- If the website loads slowly, run a speed test using Speedtest.net or a similar service. Zoom requires at least **1.5 Mbps upload/download speed** for a stable connection.

- If your connection is slow, restart your router and modem.

1.2 Switch to a Wired Connection

Wi-Fi networks can be unstable, especially in crowded areas. If possible, connect your computer to the internet using an Ethernet cable for a more stable experience.

1.3 Move Closer to the Router

If you are using Wi-Fi, ensure that you are close to the router and minimize obstructions like walls and furniture, which can weaken the signal.

1.4 Disconnect Other Devices

Other devices connected to your network (such as smartphones, tablets, or gaming consoles) may consume bandwidth. Try disconnecting unnecessary devices while attending a Zoom meeting.

1.5 Use Mobile Data as a Backup

If your Wi-Fi is down, you can use your mobile phone's hotspot as an alternative. However, keep in mind that mobile data may have limitations depending on your carrier's plan.

---

2. Incorrect Meeting Credentials

Another common issue occurs when users enter the wrong Meeting ID or Passcode, preventing them from joining a session.

Symptoms:

- Zoom displays "Invalid Meeting ID" or "Incorrect Passcode" errors.

- The meeting link does not work when clicked.

- The meeting is scheduled at a different time or has already ended.

Solutions:

2.1 Double-Check the Meeting ID and Passcode

- Ensure that you have entered the correct **Meeting ID** and **Passcode** exactly as provided by the host.

- Copy and paste the credentials instead of typing them manually to avoid errors.

2.2 Use the Direct Meeting Link

- Instead of entering the Meeting ID manually, click the **invitation link** provided by the host.

- If the link does not work, try copying and pasting it into your web browser.

2.3 Confirm the Meeting Time and Date

- Some meetings have specific start times, and you may be trying to join too early or too late.

- Check your **email invitation** or **calendar event** to confirm the scheduled time.

2.4 Request a New Invitation from the Host

If you are still unable to join, contact the host and ask for a fresh invitation link. They can also check if the meeting settings are configured correctly.

---

3. Audio and Video Not Working Upon Joining

Even if you successfully join a Zoom meeting, you might face issues where your microphone or camera does not work properly.

Symptoms:

- Other participants cannot hear you, or you cannot hear them.

- Your video does not display, or Zoom cannot detect your camera.

- The microphone or camera options are disabled in Zoom.

Solutions:

3.1 Check Audio Settings

- Click on the **microphone icon** in Zoom and ensure that it is not muted.

- Go to **Settings > Audio**, select the correct **input (microphone)** and **output (speakers/headphones)** device.

- Test your microphone by clicking **"Test Mic"** to check if Zoom detects your voice.

3.2 Check Video Settings

- Click on the **video icon** and ensure that the camera is enabled.

- In **Settings > Video**, select the correct camera from the dropdown list.

- If Zoom says "No Camera Detected," restart your device and try again.

3.3 Restart Zoom and Your Device

- Close Zoom completely and reopen it.

- Restart your computer or mobile device to refresh its system settings.

---

4. Zoom App and Software Compatibility Issues

Outdated Zoom software or incompatible system settings can also cause joining issues.

Symptoms:

- Zoom crashes upon joining.

- You receive a message saying, "Your version of Zoom is outdated."

- The meeting fails to launch, or the application is unresponsive.

Solutions:

4.1 Update Zoom to the Latest Version

- Open Zoom and go to **Settings > Check for Updates** to install the latest version.

- If you are using a mobile device, update Zoom from the **App Store (iOS)** or **Google Play Store (Android)**.

4.2 Reinstall Zoom

- If updating does not fix the issue, uninstall Zoom and reinstall it from the official Zoom website (https://zoom.us/download).

4.3 Clear Cache and Temporary Files

- On Windows:

    o Press **Win + R**, type %appdata%\Zoom, and delete the contents of the folder.

- On Mac:

    o Open Finder, go to **~/Library/Application Support/zoom.us/**, and delete cache files.

4.4 Check System Requirements

- Ensure that your device meets the **minimum system requirements** for running Zoom smoothly.

5. Firewall and Security Restrictions

Some organizations and workplaces have strict network security settings that block Zoom connections.

Symptoms:

- Zoom shows a **"Connection Timeout"** error.

- You cannot access Zoom on a corporate or school network.

- The meeting fails to load, or specific features (like screen sharing) are restricted.

Solutions:

5.1 Use a Different Network

- If you are on a school or office network, try switching to a personal Wi-Fi or mobile hotspot.

5.2 Adjust Firewall and Antivirus Settings

- If you are using Windows, go to **Windows Defender Firewall** and allow Zoom through the firewall.

- If an antivirus program is blocking Zoom, add Zoom as an **exception** in the security settings.

5.3 Contact IT Support

If you are using a company or school account, contact your IT department to check if they have blocked Zoom and request access.

Conclusion

Joining a Zoom meeting should be a seamless experience, but occasional technical issues can arise. The key to troubleshooting is identifying the specific problem—whether it's related to internet connectivity, incorrect credentials, audio/video issues, outdated software, or network restrictions.

By following the solutions outlined in this section, users can quickly resolve common joining issues and ensure a smooth meeting experience. If problems persist, reaching out to Zoom's **official support center** (https://support.zoom.us) can provide additional assistance.

Now that you understand how to troubleshoot Zoom joining issues, let's move forward with managing and hosting meetings effectively in the next section.

2.3 Starting and Managing a Meeting

2.3.1 Starting an Instant Meeting

Introduction

An instant meeting in Zoom allows users to start a meeting immediately without prior scheduling. This feature is useful for spontaneous discussions, emergency meetings, or quick catch-ups with colleagues, friends, or clients. Unlike scheduled meetings, instant meetings generate a unique meeting ID on the spot, making them easy to initiate but requiring participants to receive an invitation link or meeting ID in real time.

In this section, we will explore how to start an instant meeting on different devices, configure essential settings, manage participants effectively, and troubleshoot common issues.

1. How to Start an Instant Meeting

1.1 Starting an Instant Meeting on the Zoom Desktop App

1. **Open the Zoom App**

   o Launch the Zoom desktop application on Windows or macOS.

   o Sign in using your Zoom credentials.

2. **Click on "New Meeting"**

   o On the home screen, locate the **"New Meeting"** button.

   o Click it to start an instant meeting immediately.

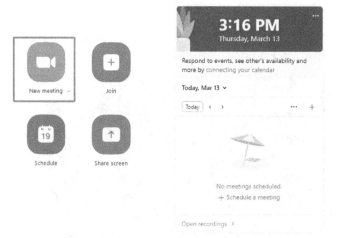

3. **Choose Your Video and Audio Preferences**

   o Before the meeting launches, Zoom provides options to start with or without video.

   o You can also select the audio settings (computer audio or phone call).

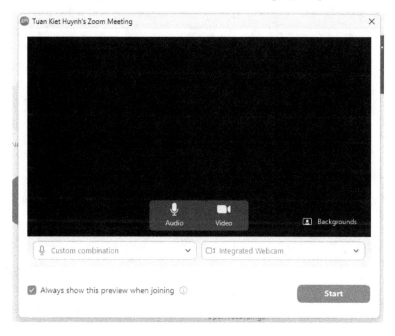

4. **Invite Participants**

○ Once inside the meeting, click on **"Participants"** in the bottom menu.

○ Click **"Invite"** to generate a link or invite people via email, contacts, or copying the meeting ID.

5. **Configure Basic Settings**

   o   Adjust your microphone and speaker settings.

   o   Enable or disable video depending on your preference.

6. **Start the Meeting and Engage Participants**

   o   Use screen sharing, chat, and other tools to facilitate the meeting.

1.2 Starting an Instant Meeting on the Zoom Mobile App

1. **Open the Zoom App**

   o   Launch the Zoom app on your mobile device (iOS or Android).

   o   Sign in with your Zoom account.

2. **Tap on "New Meeting"**

   o   On the main dashboard, tap the **"New Meeting"** button.

   o   Toggle the **"Video On"** option based on your preference.

3. **Use Your Personal Meeting ID (Optional)**

   o   If you prefer, you can enable the **Use Personal Meeting ID (PMI)** option for a consistent meeting link.

4. **Tap "Start a Meeting"**

   o   The meeting starts instantly, and you will see the video interface.

5. **Invite Participants**

   o   Tap **"Participants" > "Invite"** and share the meeting link via email, messaging apps, or copy-pasting.

1.3 Starting an Instant Meeting via the Zoom Web Portal

1. **Go to Zoom's Website**

   o   Open your web browser and navigate to zoom.us.

   o   Sign in with your account.

2. **Click on "Host a Meeting"**

- o   In the top-right corner, click **"Host a Meeting"** and select:

   - With Video On

   - With Video Off

   - Screen Share Only

3. **Launch Zoom Application**

   - o   If prompted, allow the Zoom desktop client to open.

   - o   If you don't have the app installed, you can use the web client.

4. **Invite Participants**

   - o   Click **"Participants"** > **"Invite"** and share the meeting details.

2. Essential Settings for Instant Meetings

Once the meeting has started, configuring key settings ensures a smooth experience:

Audio & Video Settings

- Mute/unmute yourself and others.

- Choose between computer audio or phone call.

- Enable virtual backgrounds for privacy.

Security & Privacy Features

- Lock the meeting to prevent unauthorized entry.

- Enable waiting rooms to control who joins.

- Remove disruptive participants if necessary.

Screen Sharing & Collaboration Tools

- Share your screen for presentations.

- Use the Whiteboard feature for brainstorming.

- Allow participants to co-host or annotate.

Recording and Transcription

- Record the meeting for future reference.

- Enable live transcription if needed.

3. Managing Participants in an Instant Meeting

Adding and Removing Participants

- Use the **"Invite"** button to add attendees.

- Remove disruptive members using the **"Remove"** option.

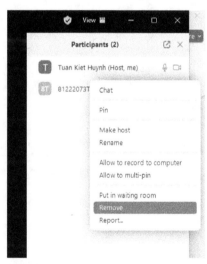

Assigning Co-Hosts and Host Controls

- Promote a participant to **Co-Host** for assistance.

- Control screen sharing permissions.

Enabling Interactive Features

- Use reactions, chat, and polling.

- Enable breakout rooms for group discussions.

4. Troubleshooting Common Issues

Connection and Audio Problems

- Check internet stability.
- Switch to a different network if needed.
- Restart Zoom or rejoin the meeting.

Video Not Working

- Ensure your camera is enabled in settings.
- Close other applications using the camera.

Unable to Share Screen

- Verify host permissions.
- Ensure screen-sharing settings are enabled.

5. Best Practices for Running an Effective Instant Meeting

Preparing Before the Meeting

- Have an agenda ready.
- Check audio and video quality.

Engaging Participants

- Encourage participation using chat and reactions.
- Use polls or Q&A sessions.

Concluding the Meeting

- Summarize key points before ending.
- Provide next steps or follow-up actions.

Conclusion

Starting an instant meeting in Zoom is a quick and efficient way to connect with others without prior scheduling. By understanding how to initiate, manage, and troubleshoot an instant meeting, users can ensure smooth communication and collaboration.

This guide has covered the necessary steps, essential settings, participant management, troubleshooting, and best practices. Mastering these elements will help you run effective and professional meetings on Zoom anytime, anywhere.

2.3.2 Enabling Waiting Rooms and Passcodes

When hosting a Zoom meeting, security is a crucial aspect that ensures only authorized participants can join. Two essential security features provided by Zoom are **Waiting Rooms** and **Passcodes**. These features help prevent unauthorized access, protect sensitive discussions, and maintain a controlled meeting environment. In this section, we will explore how to enable and configure these features, their benefits, best practices, and troubleshooting common issues.

1. Understanding Waiting Rooms and Passcodes

Before we dive into the setup process, it is essential to understand what **Waiting Rooms** and **Passcodes** do and how they differ:

- **Waiting Room:** This feature allows hosts to screen participants before they enter the meeting. Attendees who join the meeting are placed in a virtual "lobby" and must be admitted by the host or a co-host.

- **Passcodes:** A passcode (formerly called a password) is a security measure that requires participants to enter a specific code before joining a meeting. This helps ensure that only those who have received the passcode can access the session.

By using both of these features, you significantly enhance the security of your Zoom meetings.

2. How to Enable Waiting Rooms in Zoom

The **Waiting Room** feature can be enabled either for all meetings by default or for specific scheduled meetings.

2.1 Enabling the Waiting Room for All Meetings

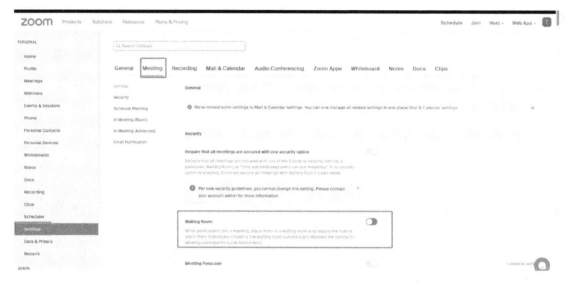

1. Sign in to Zoom: Go to the Zoom Web Portal and log in to your account.

2. Access Settings: Click on Settings in the left-side menu.

3. Navigate to Security Settings: Scroll down to the Waiting Room option.

4. Enable the Feature: Toggle the switch to turn on the Waiting Room.

5. Customize Waiting Room Settings: Click Edit Options to adjust who is placed in the waiting room (e.g., everyone or just external participants).

2.2 Enabling the Waiting Room for a Specific Meeting

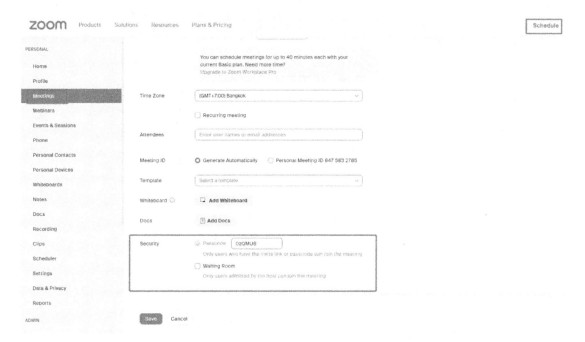

If you don't want to enable Waiting Rooms for every meeting, you can activate it for individual meetings:

1. Schedule a Meeting: Go to the Meetings tab and click Schedule a New Meeting.

2. Scroll to Security Options: Find the Waiting Room checkbox and enable it.

3. Save the Meeting Settings: Click Save to finalize your meeting configuration.

2.3 Admitting Participants from the Waiting Room

Once participants join the meeting, the host receives a notification and can admit them manually:

1. Click the **Participants** button in the Zoom toolbar.

2. Locate the participant(s) in the Waiting Room.

3. Click **Admit** to allow them into the meeting.

4. Alternatively, click **Admit All** to let everyone in at once.

2.4 Customizing the Waiting Room Experience

Zoom allows you to personalize the **Waiting Room** message to provide instructions or welcome participants:

1. In the **Waiting Room settings**, click **Customize Waiting Room**.

2. Edit the title, message, and logo that participants see while waiting.

3. Save your changes.

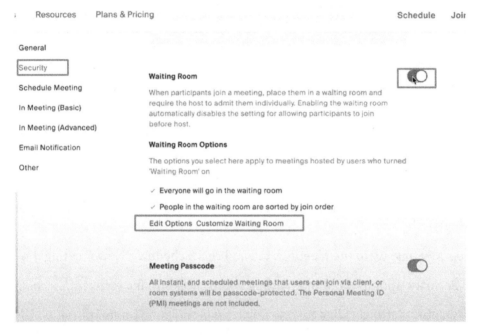

This feature is useful for branding, providing meeting instructions, or setting expectations.

3. How to Enable Passcodes for Zoom Meetings

3.1 Enabling Passcodes for All Meetings

To require passcodes for all scheduled and instant meetings:

1. Sign in to the Zoom Web Portal. https://www.zoom.com/

2. Go to **Settings > Security**.

3. Find the **Require a Passcode for Scheduled and Instant Meetings** option and toggle it on.

Now, every new meeting you create will require a passcode by default.

3.2 Enabling a Passcode for a Specific Meeting

If you prefer to set a passcode for only certain meetings:

1. When scheduling a new meeting, scroll to the **Security** section.

2. Check the **Passcode** box and enter a custom code or use the system-generated one.

3. Share the passcode along with the meeting link to invited participants.

3.3 Joining a Meeting with a Passcode

When a passcode is required, participants must enter it before they can join:

- If they click on the invitation link, the passcode is often embedded in the URL for convenience.

- If they manually enter the Meeting ID, they must type the passcode before gaining access.

---

4. Best Practices for Using Waiting Rooms and Passcodes

To maximize security while maintaining ease of access, consider the following best practices:

When to Use a Waiting Room

- For high-security meetings (e.g., legal discussions, financial meetings).

- When hosting a public webinar, allowing only approved attendees.

- When managing a classroom setting, admitting students one by one.

When to Use a Passcode

- When sending invitations broadly, ensuring only invited guests join.

- For regular team meetings, where participants already have the passcode saved.

- For client or confidential meetings, to add an extra layer of protection.

Combining Both for Maximum Security

For the highest level of security, use both the Waiting Room and a Passcode together. This ensures:

- Unauthorized users cannot join without the passcode.

- Even if they obtain the passcode, they still need to be admitted manually.

---

5. Troubleshooting Common Issues

Despite their benefits, some users may experience difficulties with these security features. Here's how to resolve them:

Participants Stuck in the Waiting Room

- **Issue:** Participants are not getting admitted.

- **Solution:** Ensure the host or co-host is actively monitoring the Waiting Room. If auto-admit is enabled, check the settings.

Participants Cannot Join Due to Passcode Issues

- **Issue:** Attendees report that the passcode is not working.

- **Solution:** Verify that the passcode was copied correctly. If issues persist, try removing special characters from the passcode.

Embedded Passcode Link Not Working

- **Issue:** Participants click the link but still get asked for a passcode.

- **Solution:** Check if the meeting settings include the embedded passcode feature. If needed, resend the correct invitation link.

Managing Large Numbers of Participants in the Waiting Room

- **Issue:** Handling a high volume of attendees manually can be challenging.

- **Solution:** Assign co-hosts to help monitor the Waiting Room and admit participants.

6. Conclusion

Enabling Waiting Rooms and Passcodes is a crucial step in securing your Zoom meetings. While passcodes add a barrier to entry, Waiting Rooms provide additional control over who gets admitted. By leveraging these features correctly, you can:

- Prevent unauthorized access.

- Maintain a professional and secure meeting environment.

- Ensure that only the right participants join your meetings.

By following the setup guides, best practices, and troubleshooting steps in this chapter, you can confidently use Zoom's security features to host safe and productive virtual meetings.

2.3.3 Managing Participants

Managing participants effectively is crucial for running a smooth and productive Zoom meeting. As a host or co-host, you have several tools at your disposal to maintain control, ensure engagement, and handle disruptions. This section will cover everything you need to know about managing participants, including participant controls, interaction settings, and best practices for maintaining an organized meeting.

1. Understanding Participant Roles in Zoom

Before diving into participant management, it's essential to understand the different roles available in a Zoom meeting. Each role has specific permissions that affect what actions a user can take.

1.1 Host

The host is the person who schedules and starts the meeting. They have full control over all meeting settings and participant actions. Some of the key responsibilities of a host include:

- Admitting participants from the waiting room.
- Muting and unmuting attendees.
- Assigning co-hosts.
- Removing disruptive participants.
- Ending the meeting for everyone.

1.2 Co-Host

A co-host has many of the same privileges as the host but cannot:

- Start or end the meeting.
- Manage breakout rooms.
- Assign other co-hosts.

Co-hosts are useful for assisting with large meetings, especially when managing multiple participants.

1.3 Participants

Regular participants are attendees in the meeting with limited controls. They can:

- Mute and unmute themselves (if allowed).
- Share their screen (if permitted).
- Send chat messages.
- Use reactions and raise their hand.

1.4 Alternative Host

An alternative host is assigned before the meeting starts and can start the meeting in the host's absence. This role is useful for backup planning if the primary host cannot attend.

2. Accessing the Participant List and Controls

To manage participants, you need to access the **Participants Panel** in Zoom.

2.1 Opening the Participants Panel

1. In an active Zoom meeting, click on **Participants** in the meeting toolbar.

2. A panel will appear on the right side (or as a separate window on mobile), displaying the list of participants and available controls.

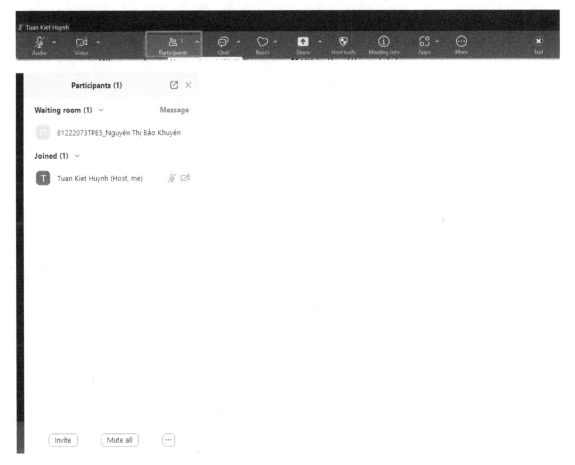

2.2 Host and Co-Host Controls

When you hover over a participant's name, a **More** button (three dots) appears, giving you additional options:

- **Mute/Unmute:** Control a participant's microphone.

- **Stop Video:** Disable a participant's video feed.

- **Make Host/Co-Host:** Promote another user to help manage the meeting.

- **Remove Participant:** Eject someone from the meeting.

- **Rename:** Change a participant's display name.

- **Put in Waiting Room:** Temporarily move a participant out of the meeting.

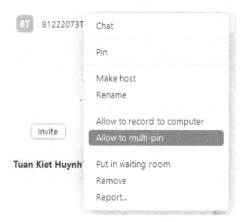

3. Managing Participant Audio and Video

3.1 Muting and Unmuting Participants

In large meetings, background noise can be disruptive. The host can mute all participants at once by:

1. Clicking **Participants** to open the panel.

2. Selecting **Mute All** at the bottom of the panel.

3. Choosing whether to allow participants to unmute themselves.

To unmute individuals, the host can:

- Click **Ask to Unmute** on a specific participant.

- Enable the setting **Allow Participants to Unmute Themselves** if desired.

3.2 Controlling Video Permissions

Hosts can stop a participant's video if needed:

- Click **Stop Video** next to the participant's name.

- The participant can turn it back on unless the host locks video settings.

For larger meetings or sensitive discussions, consider disabling video for all participants at the beginning.

4. Managing Chat and Reactions

4.1 Controlling Chat Access

The chat feature allows participants to communicate during a meeting. As a host, you can manage chat settings by:

1. Clicking **Chat** in the meeting toolbar.

2. Clicking the three-dot menu to adjust chat permissions:

    o **Everyone:** All participants can send messages.

    o **Host and Co-Host Only:** Participants can only message the host.

      o   **Disabled:** Turns off chat for everyone.

4.2 Using Reactions and Hand Raising

Zoom reactions allow participants to engage non-verbally using emojis like thumbs-up 👍 or clapping 👏. The "Raise Hand" feature is useful in structured discussions. To manage raised hands:

- Open the **Participants Panel** and look for the raised hand icon.

- Call on participants in order.

- Click **Lower Hand** when they are done speaking.

5. Handling Disruptions and Security Settings

Enabling the Waiting Room

To prevent unauthorized users from joining, use the **Waiting Room** feature:

1. Open **Security** in the toolbar.

2. Enable **Waiting Room** to manually admit participants.

This prevents "Zoombombing" (unwanted intrusions).

Locking the Meeting

Once all expected participants have joined, you can **lock the meeting**:

- Click **Security > Lock Meeting**

- No new participants can join until it's unlocked.

Removing Disruptive Participants

If someone is disruptive, remove them by:

1. Clicking **Participants** and finding their name.

2. Clicking **More > Remove**

3. Once removed, they **cannot** rejoin unless allowed.

6. Assigning Co-Hosts and Breakout Room Moderators

Making Someone a Co-Host

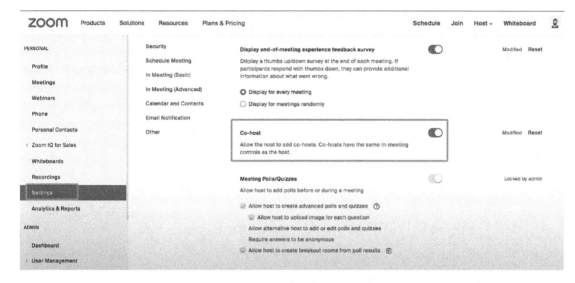

If you need help managing the meeting, assign a **co-host**:

- Click **Participants**

- Find the user, click **More**, and select **Make Co-Host**

7. Best Practices for Managing Participants

Setting Meeting Rules

Before starting, communicate meeting etiquette:

- Keep microphones muted when not speaking.
- Raise a hand before speaking.
- Use the chat for questions.

Engaging Participants

To keep participants involved:

- Call on attendees by name.
- Use polls and Q&A sessions.
- Rotate speakers to maintain attention.

Handling Large Meetings

For meetings with **100+ participants**:

- Assign multiple **co-hosts**.
- Use **Breakout Rooms** for smaller discussions.
- Pre-set **mute all** to minimize background noise.

Conclusion

Managing participants in Zoom is an essential skill for hosting productive meetings. By understanding participant roles, controlling audio and video, managing chat, and handling disruptions, you can ensure a seamless experience for everyone. Using features like co-hosts, breakout rooms, and security settings will help maintain order and engagement.

By implementing these best practices, you'll create a professional, interactive, and well-organized Zoom meeting environment, whether for business, education, or personal use.

CHAPTER III
Using Zoom Meeting Features

3.1 Audio and Video Controls

3.1.1 Adjusting Microphone and Speaker Settings

Introduction

Audio quality is one of the most critical factors for a smooth and productive Zoom meeting. Clear and reliable audio ensures that participants can effectively communicate without distractions caused by poor sound. In this section, we will explore how to adjust microphone and speaker settings in Zoom, troubleshoot common audio issues, and optimize your setup for the best meeting experience.

1. Accessing Audio Settings in Zoom

Before adjusting microphone and speaker settings, you need to access the Zoom audio settings menu. Here's how:

On the Desktop App (Windows/Mac)

1. **Open Zoom** and click on your profile picture in the top-right corner.

2. Select **"Settings"** from the dropdown menu.

3. Navigate to the **"Audio"** tab in the left sidebar.

During a Zoom Meeting

1. Click on the small arrow (^) next to the **microphone icon** in the meeting toolbar.

2. Select **"Audio Settings..."** to open the configuration window.

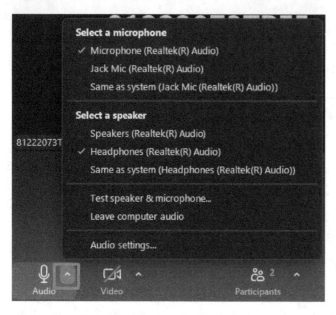

On Mobile (iOS/Android)

1. Open the Zoom app and tap on **"Settings"** in the bottom menu.

2. Select **"Meetings"** and then navigate to the **"Audio"** section.

Once inside the audio settings, you can fine-tune your microphone and speaker configurations to enhance your audio experience.

---

2. Choosing the Right Microphone and Speaker

Zoom allows users to select their preferred microphone and speaker devices. This is useful for those using external audio equipment, such as USB microphones, Bluetooth headsets, or professional sound systems.

How to Select a Microphone in Zoom

1. Go to **Zoom Audio Settings** as explained earlier.

2. Under the **Microphone** section, click on the dropdown menu to see available devices.

3. Select your preferred microphone (e.g., built-in laptop microphone, USB microphone, external headset).

4. Click **"Test Mic"** to ensure that Zoom detects your voice.

How to Select a Speaker in Zoom

1. In the **Audio Settings** tab, navigate to the **Speaker** section.

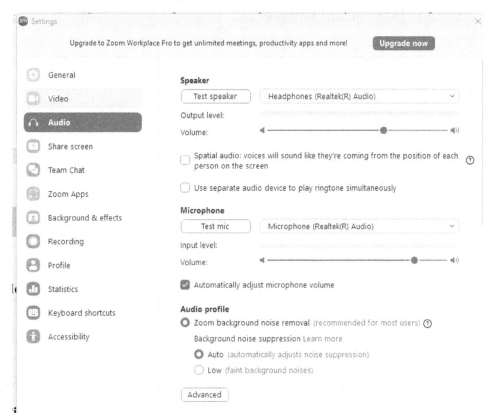

2. Click on the dropdown menu and choose your preferred output device (e.g., built-in laptop speakers, Bluetooth headset, external speakers).

3. Click **"Test Speaker"** to check if the audio output is working correctly.

Tip: If you are using an external microphone or headset, ensure it is properly connected before starting your Zoom meeting.

3. Adjusting Microphone Volume and Sensitivity

Automatic vs. Manual Volume Adjustment

Zoom provides an **"Automatically adjust microphone volume"** feature, which dynamically changes the microphone sensitivity based on your speaking volume. However, in some cases, manually setting the microphone volume is preferable for consistent sound quality.

How to Manually Adjust Microphone Volume

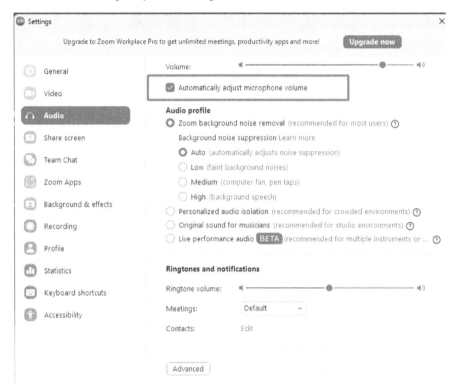

1. Open **Zoom Audio Settings**.

2. Under the **Microphone** section, uncheck **"Automatically adjust microphone volume"**.

3. Move the volume slider to increase or decrease microphone sensitivity.

4. Click **"Test Mic"** and speak into your microphone to find the optimal volume level.

Best Practices for Setting Microphone Volume

- Keep the volume at a medium level to avoid distortion.

- If others say your voice is too loud or too soft, adjust the slider accordingly.

- For external microphones, adjust gain levels directly on the device (if applicable).

4. Enhancing Audio Quality with Noise Suppression

Background noise can disrupt a meeting and make communication difficult. Zoom includes a built-in **noise suppression** feature to minimize unwanted sounds such as keyboard typing, fan noise, and background chatter.

Adjusting Noise Suppression Levels

1. Open **Zoom Audio Settings**.

2. Scroll to the **"Suppress background noise"** section.

3. Choose from the following options:

   o **Auto** (default): Zoom automatically adjusts noise suppression.

   o **Low**: Reduces minor background noise while preserving voice clarity.

   o **Medium**: Suppresses moderate background sounds.

   o **High**: Strong noise suppression but may slightly distort voice quality.

Tip: If you are in a quiet environment, selecting **"Low"** may improve voice clarity.

5. Using Zoom's Advanced Audio Settings

For users who want greater control over their audio experience, Zoom offers **Advanced Audio Settings**, accessible via:

1. **Zoom Audio Settings** → Click **"Advanced"** (bottom right corner).

Key Advanced Audio Features

- **"Echo Cancellation"**: Reduces echo when using built-in laptop speakers.

- **"High-Fidelity Music Mode"**: Optimizes audio for live music performances.

- **"Stereo Audio"**: Enables stereo sound for a richer listening experience.

- **"Original Sound for Musicians"**: Bypasses Zoom's audio processing for studio-quality sound.

Tip: These settings are useful for musicians, podcasters, and users hosting high-quality audio events.

---

6. Troubleshooting Common Audio Issues

Despite adjusting settings, users may experience audio problems. Here's how to resolve them:

Problem 1: No Sound from Microphone

Solution:

- Ensure your microphone is selected in Zoom settings.
- Check that the microphone is **not muted** (press **Alt + A** to toggle mute).
- Restart Zoom or reconnect your external microphone.

Problem 2: Participants Can't Hear You Clearly

Solution:

- Increase microphone volume in **Audio Settings**.
- Use a wired headset for clearer sound.
- Enable **"High-fidelity music mode"** for better audio quality.

Problem 3: Echo or Feedback Noise

Solution:

- Use headphones instead of speakers to prevent feedback.
- Enable **"Echo Cancellation"** in Advanced Audio Settings.
- Ask participants to mute themselves when not speaking.

Problem 4: Audio Lag or Delay

Solution:

- Close background applications using internet bandwidth.
- Use a wired internet connection for stability.

- Reduce Zoom's audio processing by disabling **"Background Noise Suppression"**.

---

7. Final Tips for a Great Audio Experience

To ensure the best audio experience in Zoom meetings, follow these tips:

✓ Use a quality external microphone for professional sound.

✓ Find a quiet environment to minimize background noise.

✓ Test your audio setup before important meetings.

✓ Encourage participants to mute when not speaking.

✓ Keep Zoom updated to access the latest audio features.

By properly adjusting microphone and speaker settings, users can significantly improve their communication in Zoom meetings. A well-optimized audio setup leads to clearer discussions, fewer misunderstandings, and more productive virtual collaborations.

3.1.2 Managing Video Settings and Backgrounds

Introduction

Video quality plays a crucial role in creating a professional and engaging Zoom meeting experience. Whether you're attending a business meeting, teaching a class, or catching up with friends, adjusting your video settings can significantly impact how you are perceived. Zoom offers a variety of customization options for video settings, including camera selection, resolution adjustments, lighting enhancements, and virtual backgrounds. This section will guide you through managing these settings effectively to enhance your presence in any Zoom meeting.

---

1. Accessing Video Settings in Zoom

Before making any adjustments, you need to access Zoom's video settings. Follow these steps:

1. Open the Zoom desktop client or mobile app.

2. Click on your profile picture in the top-right corner and select **"Settings"** (or go to the gear icon in the main menu).

3. In the settings panel, select **"Video"** from the left-hand menu.

4. A preview of your camera feed will appear along with various customization options.

Alternatively, you can access video settings during a meeting:

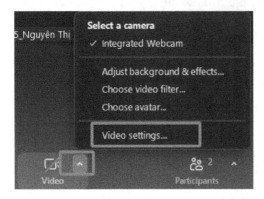

- Click on the **upward arrow (^)** next to the **"Start Video"** button on the meeting toolbar.

- Select **"Video Settings"** to open the same menu.

2. Choosing and Adjusting Your Camera

Selecting the Right Camera

If your device has multiple cameras (e.g., an external webcam and a built-in laptop camera), you can select which one to use:

- In the **Video Settings** menu, click the **"Camera"** dropdown.

- Choose the camera that provides the best quality.

- If you are using an external webcam, ensure it is connected properly before selecting it in Zoom.

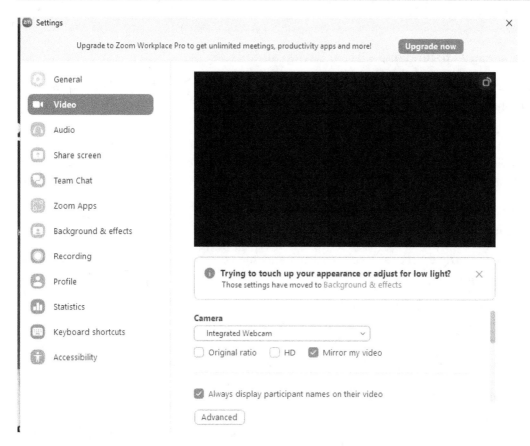

Adjusting Camera Quality

Zoom automatically adjusts video resolution based on your internet connection, but you can improve video clarity by:

- Ensuring your webcam supports **HD video** (720p or 1080p).

- Checking **"Enable HD"** in Zoom's video settings (if available in your plan).

- Using **"Adjust for low light"** to brighten the image in dim conditions.

Optimizing Lighting and Positioning

- Face a natural light source or use a ring light to reduce shadows.

- Position your camera at **eye level** for a natural and engaging view.

- Avoid backlighting from windows, which can cause overexposure.

3. Enabling and Customizing Virtual Backgrounds

Zoom allows users to replace their background with an image or video, which can enhance professionalism and privacy.

How to Enable Virtual Backgrounds

1. Open **Video Settings** and go to **"Background & Effects"** (formerly called "Virtual Background").

2. Check **"I have a green screen"** if using a physical green screen (optional but improves quality).

3. Click **"Choose Virtual Background"** and select a default background or upload a custom image/video.

Recommended Image and Video Requirements

-   **Images:** Minimum resolution of 1280x720 pixels for best quality.

-   **Videos:** MP4 or MOV format, with a resolution of at least 1080p.

Using Zoom's Blur Background Feature

For those who prefer not to use an artificial background but still want privacy:

-   Select **"Blur"** under virtual backgrounds to softly blur everything behind you.

4. Advanced Video Filters and Effects

Zoom offers video filters and touch-up options to enhance appearance.

Using Video Filters

-   In **Background & Effects**, select **"Video Filters"** to add fun overlays (e.g., black-and-white mode or seasonal themes).

-   These filters are useful for casual meetings or creative presentations.

Applying the Touch-Up Appearance Feature

-   Go to **Video Settings** and enable **"Touch up my appearance"** to smooth facial features.

- Adjust the slider to control the level of effect applied.

- This feature works well for professional settings, subtly improving video quality without looking artificial.

5. Using Studio Effects (Eyebrows, Mustache, Lip Color)

For further customization, Zoom provides **Studio Effects** that let you enhance facial features.

- Access **"Background & Effects"** and click **"Studio Effects (Beta)"** at the bottom.

- Choose from options like eyebrow shapes, mustaches, and lip colors.

- These settings can be saved as a default for future meetings.

6. Troubleshooting Common Video Issues

Even with the best settings, users may encounter video-related problems.

6.1 Camera Not Detected

Solutions:

- Ensure your camera is properly connected (if external).

- Restart your device and reopen Zoom.

- Check for software conflicts (e.g., close other apps that might be using the camera, such as Skype or Teams).

6.2 Video Lagging or Freezing

Causes:

- Poor internet connection.

- High CPU usage.

Fixes:

- Reduce resolution by disabling **HD video** in settings.

- Close unnecessary applications running in the background.

- Use a wired connection instead of Wi-Fi for stability.

6.3 Green Screen or Background Issues

Fixes:

- Use a plain, solid-colored background for better effect.

- Ensure good lighting to improve Zoom's ability to differentiate you from the background.

- If the virtual background appears patchy, disable **"I have a green screen"** unless you're using an actual one.

7. Best Practices for Professional Video Setup

To ensure you always look your best in Zoom meetings, follow these expert recommendations:

Keep Your Camera at Eye Level

- Position your webcam so your face is centered.

- Avoid extreme angles that can be unflattering.

Ensure Good Lighting

- Use soft, even lighting from the front.

- Avoid direct overhead lighting that can create harsh shadows.

Choose an Appropriate Background

- Use a tidy, neutral background or a professional virtual background.

- Avoid distracting elements like cluttered rooms or moving objects.

Wear Solid-Colored Clothing

- Avoid patterned or reflective outfits that may interfere with virtual backgrounds.

- Choose neutral or darker colors for a professional look.

Conclusion

Managing video settings in Zoom can significantly enhance your meeting experience by improving video quality, ensuring privacy, and creating a more engaging presence. By selecting the right camera, adjusting lighting, using virtual backgrounds effectively, and applying advanced video features, you can project a professional and polished image in every meeting.

With Zoom's continuous updates, it's essential to stay informed about new video features and best practices. Mastering these settings will allow you to participate confidently in any virtual meeting, whether for business, education, or social gatherings.

3.1.3 Muting and Unmuting Participants

In any Zoom meeting, managing audio is crucial to maintaining a professional and organized session. Whether you're hosting a large webinar, a team meeting, or an online class, knowing how to **mute and unmute participants** effectively can improve communication, reduce distractions, and ensure a smoother experience for everyone involved.

This section will cover:

- How to mute and unmute yourself
- How to mute and unmute participants as a host or co-host
- Managing audio settings for a productive meeting
- Common issues and troubleshooting

Muting and Unmuting Yourself

As a participant in a Zoom meeting, you have full control over your own microphone. This means you can mute and unmute yourself whenever necessary to contribute to the discussion or minimize background noise.

How to Mute and Unmute Yourself

There are multiple ways to mute or unmute yourself in Zoom:

1. **Using the Zoom toolbar**

   o   Look at the bottom-left corner of your screen.

   o   Click on the **microphone icon** to mute or unmute yourself.

   o   A red slash across the microphone indicates you are muted.

2. **Using keyboard shortcuts**

   o   **Windows:** Press **Alt + A** to toggle mute/unmute.

   o   **Mac:** Press **Command + Shift + A** to toggle mute/unmute.

3. **Holding down the spacebar (Push-to-Talk feature)**

   o   If you are muted, you can press and hold the **spacebar** to temporarily unmute yourself while speaking.

   o   Once you release the spacebar, you will be muted again.

4. **From the Participants Panel**

   o   Click on **Participants** in the Zoom toolbar.

   o   Find your name and click **Unmute** or **Mute** next to it.

Best Practices for Muting Yourself

- **Mute yourself when not speaking** to prevent background noise from disrupting the meeting.

- **Test your microphone** before the meeting to ensure clear audio.

- **Use the spacebar for quick responses** instead of toggling the mute button repeatedly.

- **Check the mute icon** before speaking to avoid talking while muted.

Muting and Unmuting Participants as a Host or Co-Host

As a **host** or **co-host**, you have the ability to control the audio of other participants. This is especially useful for large meetings, webinars, or classrooms where background noise can be a major issue.

How to Mute a Single Participant

1. **Using the Participants Panel**

   o Click on **Participants** in the Zoom toolbar.

   o Find the participant's name in the list.

   o Click on **Mute** next to their name.

2. **Using Right-Click Options**

   o If their video is on, right-click their video feed.

   o Click **Mute Audio**.

3. **From the Meeting Window**

   o Hover over the participant's video or name.

   o Click the **More (•••) button**.

   o Select **Mute**.

How to Unmute a Single Participant

1. **Using the Participants Panel**

   o Click on **Participants**.

   o Find the muted participant's name.

   o Click **Ask to Unmute** (Participants must manually unmute themselves).

2. **Using Right-Click Options**

    o   Right-click on the participant's video.

    o   Select **Ask to Unmute**.

Note: Due to privacy settings, Zoom does not allow a host to unmute participants directly without their permission. Instead, Zoom will send them a prompt asking them to unmute themselves.

Muting and Unmuting All Participants

In some cases, it's useful to mute **everyone at once**, especially in large meetings where multiple people may accidentally leave their microphones on.

How to Mute All Participants at Once

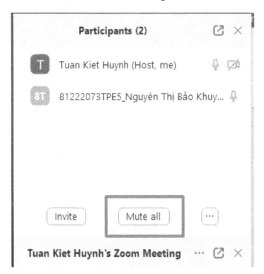

1. Click on **Participants** in the Zoom toolbar.

2. At the bottom of the Participants panel, click **Mute All**.

3. A pop-up will appear asking if you want to allow participants to unmute themselves.

    o   **If checked**, participants can unmute themselves anytime.

    o   **If unchecked**, only the host or co-host can unmute them.

How to Unmute All Participants

1. Click on **Participants** in the Zoom toolbar.

2. Click **Unmute All**.

3. A request will be sent to all participants, and they must manually unmute themselves.

Advanced Audio Controls for Muting

Zoom provides additional settings that allow hosts to control participant audio behavior more effectively.

Preventing Participants from Unmuting Themselves

If you want full control over the audio, you can prevent participants from unmuting themselves.

1. Click **Participants** in the Zoom toolbar.

2. Click the **More (•••) button** at the bottom of the panel.

3. Select **Allow Participants to Unmute Themselves** to toggle this setting on or off.

When this option is disabled, only the host or co-host can unmute participants manually.

Muting Upon Entry

For large meetings, it is helpful to mute participants as soon as they join to avoid disruptions.

1. Click **Participants** in the Zoom toolbar.

2. Click **More (•••)** at the bottom of the panel.

3. Select **Mute Participants Upon Entry**.

Managing Audio Permissions in Webinars

In Zoom **Webinars**, attendees are **muted by default** and cannot unmute themselves. Only the host, co-host, or panelists can speak. Hosts can:

- Promote an attendee to **Panelist** to allow them to speak.

- Use the **Unmute Request** to let an attendee unmute themselves.

Common Issues and Troubleshooting

While managing audio in Zoom is straightforward, users may sometimes encounter technical issues. Here are some common problems and their solutions:

1. "I can't unmute myself"

- Check if the host has disabled participant unmuting.

- Ensure that your microphone is not muted at the system level (Windows or macOS).

- Try leaving and rejoining the meeting.

2. "My microphone isn't working"

- Click the **arrow next to the microphone icon** and select the correct input device.

- Restart your computer or check microphone permissions in system settings.

3. "Other participants can't hear me"

- Make sure you are unmuted in Zoom.

- Increase your microphone volume in Zoom's **Audio Settings**.

- Test your microphone in **Zoom > Settings > Audio > Test Mic**.

4. "Background noise is too loud"

- Use **Zoom's noise suppression** feature in **Settings > Audio**.

- Mute participants who have disruptive background noise.

5. "Echo or audio feedback is occurring"

- Ensure no one has multiple devices in the same room using Zoom.

- Ask participants to **use headphones** to reduce echo.

- Lower speaker volume to minimize feedback loops.

Final Tips for Effective Audio Management

- **As a participant**, always mute yourself when not speaking.

- **As a host or co-host**, be proactive in muting participants to prevent disruptions.

- **Use keyboard shortcuts** for quick mute/unmute actions.

- **Familiarize yourself with Zoom's advanced audio controls** to manage large meetings effectively.

- **Encourage proper microphone use** for better communication quality.

By mastering these muting and unmuting features, you can ensure a seamless, distraction-free meeting experience on Zoom.

3.2 Screen Sharing and Presenting

3.2.1 Sharing Your Screen

Screen sharing is one of the most powerful and widely used features in Zoom. It allows hosts and participants to share their computer screens, presentations, documents, and applications in real time. Whether you're conducting a business meeting, teaching an online class, or presenting a project, knowing how to effectively share your screen can enhance communication and engagement.

Understanding Screen Sharing in Zoom

Screen sharing enables users to display their desktop or specific applications to other participants in a Zoom meeting. This feature is particularly useful for:

- Presenting slideshows or documents (e.g., PowerPoint, Google Slides, PDFs).

- Demonstrating software or applications during training sessions.

- Collaborating on files with teams in real-time.

- Showing videos with sound for educational or entertainment purposes.

Who Can Share Their Screen?

By default, the host controls who can share their screen. The host can:

- Allow all participants to share their screen.

- Restrict screen sharing to only the host.

- Enable screen sharing for specific individuals.

Understanding these settings ensures that screen sharing is used appropriately in different meeting scenarios.

How to Share Your Screen in Zoom

Step 1: Starting Screen Sharing

1. **Join or Start a Zoom Meeting**

   o Open Zoom and either join an existing meeting or start a new one as a host.

2. **Click on the 'Share Screen' Button**

   o At the bottom of the Zoom meeting window, click on the green **"Share Screen"** button.

3. **Select What You Want to Share**

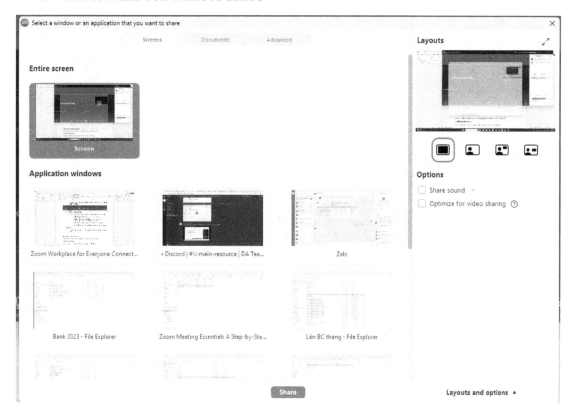

   o A pop-up window will appear with different sharing options, including:

   ▪ **Entire Screen** – Shares everything on your monitor.

- **Specific Application Window** – Shares only the selected application (e.g., PowerPoint, Word, or Chrome).

- **Whiteboard** – Opens a digital whiteboard for collaboration.

- **iPhone/iPad via AirPlay or Cable** – Shares a mobile device screen.

4. **Click 'Share'**

   o Once you select your preferred sharing option, click the **"Share"** button to start.

Types of Screen Sharing Options

Zoom provides various screen-sharing options tailored to different needs.

1. Full Screen Sharing

This option shares everything visible on your screen. It is ideal for:

- Teaching lessons that require switching between multiple applications.

- Providing step-by-step software demonstrations.

- Showing web-based content that needs real-time navigation.

✦ **Tip:** If you have multiple monitors, Zoom will allow you to choose which screen to share.

2. Application Window Sharing

When you choose this option, only the selected application is shared. Participants won't see other windows or notifications. It's useful for:

- Keeping distractions to a minimum.

- Protecting sensitive information from being displayed accidentally.

- Sharing a single document or program without revealing your desktop.

3. Whiteboard Sharing

The Zoom **Whiteboard** allows users to write, draw, and brainstorm in real time. It's especially useful for:

- Interactive teaching and tutoring.

- Visualizing concepts during meetings.

- Taking collaborative notes.

4. iPhone/iPad Screen Sharing

Zoom enables users to share their iPhone or iPad screens via AirPlay or a physical cable connection. This is beneficial for:

- Demonstrating mobile apps.

- Teaching iPad-based digital art or note-taking.

- Presenting from a mobile device.

Optimizing Screen Sharing for Presentations

To ensure a smooth and professional experience while sharing your screen, follow these best practices:

1. Close Unnecessary Applications

Before sharing your screen, close any applications that you don't need. This prevents distractions and helps improve performance.

2. Use "Share Computer Sound" for Videos

If you're playing a video or audio file, enable the **"Share Sound"** option when sharing your screen to ensure participants can hear the audio clearly.

3. Enable "Optimize for Video Clip"

For smoother video playback, check the **"Optimize for Video Clip"** box before sharing. This improves frame rates and reduces lag.

4. Use Dual Monitors if Possible

If you have two screens, you can share one while keeping your meeting controls visible on the other. This helps manage the presentation more efficiently.

5. Pause Screen Sharing When Needed

If you need to take a moment to prepare without stopping screen sharing entirely, use the **Pause Share** button. This freezes the current view for participants while you adjust your content.

6. Use Annotation Tools for Engagement

Zoom provides built-in annotation tools, allowing presenters and participants to highlight, draw, and mark up shared content.

Managing Screen Sharing Permissions

As a host, you can control screen sharing settings to maintain security and order in meetings.

1. Restricting Screen Sharing to the Host

To prevent disruptions, go to:

- **Security Icon** > Uncheck **"Allow Participants to Share Screen"**

2. Allowing Specific Participants to Share

If you want only certain attendees to share their screen:

- Click on **"Participants"**, find the person's name, click **"More"**, then select **"Make Co-Host"**.

3. Disabling Participant Annotations

If you want to prevent participants from drawing over shared content:

- Click on **"More"** (in the sharing toolbar) and disable **"Annotate on Shared Content"**.

Troubleshooting Common Screen Sharing Issues

1. Participants Cannot See Your Screen

♦ **Solution:** Ensure you've selected the correct window/application and that your Zoom app is up to date.

2. Lag or Delays During Screen Sharing

♦ **Solution:** Close unnecessary applications, reduce video resolution, and ensure a stable internet connection.

3. Audio Not Sharing with Video

♦ **Solution:** Enable **"Share Computer Sound"** before starting the screen share.

4. Screen Sharing Button is Missing

♦ **Solution:** The host may have disabled screen sharing. Ask for permission or check settings.

5. Black Screen Issue While Sharing

♦ **Solution:** Update graphics drivers and disable hardware acceleration in Zoom settings.

Final Tips for Effective Screen Sharing

✓ **Test Before Your Meeting** – Practice screen sharing in a test meeting to ensure everything works smoothly.

✓ **Use Clear Visuals** – Ensure that your slides, documents, or videos are well-organized and easy to read.

✓ **Engage with Your Audience** – Ask questions, use annotations, and encourage participants to interact.

✓ **Keep It Professional** – Turn off notifications, use a clean desktop background, and avoid multitasking during presentations.

✓ **Have a Backup Plan** – If screen sharing fails, be ready to share files via chat or email.

Conclusion

Mastering screen sharing in Zoom enhances your ability to communicate, collaborate, and present effectively. Whether you're hosting a professional meeting, conducting a webinar, or teaching a virtual class, understanding how to share your screen efficiently ensures a smoother and more engaging experience. By following best practices and troubleshooting common issues, you can make the most of Zoom's screen-sharing features and deliver impactful presentations.

3.2.2 Optimizing Video and Audio for Presentations

When delivering a presentation via Zoom, **audio and video quality** plays a crucial role in keeping your audience engaged and ensuring your message is conveyed clearly. Poor video resolution, lagging audio, or background noise can lead to frustration and a lack of focus. In this section, we will explore **how to optimize video and audio for presentations**, covering key settings, best practices, and troubleshooting tips to deliver a professional and seamless experience.

1. Video Optimization for Presentations

High-quality video enhances the **visual impact** of your presentation, ensuring that your audience remains engaged. Here's how to achieve the best video settings:

1.1 Selecting the Right Camera

- Use an external HD webcam if your built-in laptop camera has poor resolution. External cameras generally offer higher resolution, better color accuracy, and improved low-light performance.

- If using a built-in camera, ensure it is positioned at eye level to create a natural and engaging perspective.

1.2 Adjusting Video Settings in Zoom

To enhance your video quality in Zoom, navigate to:

1. Click on Settings (gear icon) in the Zoom app.

2. Select Video from the left menu.

3. Adjust the following settings:

   o Enable HD: Provides higher video quality (if your internet connection supports it).

   o Adjust for low light: Zoom automatically enhances brightness in dim conditions.

   o Touch up my appearance: Smooths skin tone for a more polished look.

   o Mirror my video: Helps ensure that text appears correctly when shown on camera.

1.3 Lighting and Background Setup

Good lighting is essential for clear video quality. Consider these tips:

- Use natural light or soft LED lights placed in front of you (not behind) to avoid shadows.

- Avoid overhead lighting, as it creates unflattering shadows on your face.

- Choose a clean and professional background or use Zoom's virtual background feature. Navigate to Settings > Background & Effects to select or upload a background.

- For better background clarity, use a green screen or an AI-powered background blur effect.

1.4 Ensuring a Stable Internet Connection

A weak internet connection can result in pixelated video or lag during your presentation. Here's how to maintain a stable connection:

- Use a wired Ethernet connection instead of Wi-Fi for better stability.

- If using Wi-Fi, position yourself close to the router and minimize background devices consuming bandwidth.

- Run a speed test to ensure your upload speed is at least 3 Mbps for HD video streaming.

2. Audio Optimization for Presentations

Clear and high-quality **audio** is even more critical than video in an online presentation. A professional-sounding presentation minimizes distractions and keeps the audience engaged.

2.1 Choosing the Right Microphone

Your microphone choice significantly impacts your audio quality:

- External USB microphones provide better clarity than built-in laptop microphones. Popular choices include the Blue Yeti, Rode NT-USB, and Audio-Technica AT2020.

- Lapel microphones (Lavalier mics) are great for hands-free speaking.

- Headset microphones reduce background noise and are ideal for loud environments.

2.2 Adjusting Audio Settings in Zoom

To optimize audio, follow these steps:

1. Open Zoom Settings and navigate to Audio.

2. Under Microphone, select your preferred mic and adjust:

    o Automatically adjust microphone volume (uncheck for manual control).

    o Suppress background noise: Set to High in noisy environments.

  o Echo cancellation: Zoom automatically reduces echo, but using headphones eliminates it entirely.

3. Under Speaker, choose high-quality speakers or headphones to avoid audio feedback.

2.3 Enabling High-Fidelity Audio for Music and Presentations

For music, high-quality recordings, or professional audio presentations, enable Original Sound for Musicians in Zoom:

1. Go to Settings > Audio.

2. Enable Show in-meeting option to enable Original Sound.

3. During the meeting, click Turn On Original Sound to bypass Zoom's automatic noise suppression.

2.4 Reducing Background Noise

Background noise can disrupt your presentation, so follow these steps to minimize it:

- Use Zoom's background noise suppression feature (Settings > Audio > Suppress Background Noise).

- Mute all unnecessary participants while presenting to prevent interruptions.

- Present in a quiet room, close windows, and silence notifications.

- Consider using AI-powered noise reduction tools like Krisp.ai for additional clarity.

2.5 Using a Second Device for Audio Monitoring

If you want to ensure your audience hears you clearly, consider using a second device:

- Join the meeting with a phone or tablet as a listener to check audio quality.

- Avoid feedback loops by muting the second device's microphone.

3. Best Practices for a Smooth Presentation

Rehearsing Before the Meeting

- Conduct a test run by recording yourself in Zoom to identify any issues with video, audio, or internet speed.

- Check your slides and animations to ensure they display properly.

- Adjust screen-sharing settings in advance (Settings > Share Screen > Optimize for full-screen video clip).

Engaging Your Audience

- Speak slowly and clearly, emphasizing key points.

- Use gestures and facial expressions to enhance communication.

- Encourage audience interaction via chat, polls, or Q&A sessions.

Troubleshooting Common Video and Audio Issues

Issue	Possible Causes	Solutions
Choppy Video	Poor internet connection	Use Ethernet, close background apps, lower video resolution
Lagging Audio	Bandwidth overload	Mute unused participants, close extra browser tabs
Echo or Feedback	Multiple devices in the same room	Use headphones, mute unnecessary devices
Background Noise	Noisy environment	Enable noise suppression, use an external mic

4. Conclusion

Optimizing video and audio quality in Zoom meetings significantly improves the effectiveness of your presentation. By selecting the right equipment, configuring Zoom settings properly, and following best practices, you can **ensure a smooth and professional experience** for both you and your audience.

Key takeaways from this section:

✓ Invest in **high-quality cameras and microphones** for the best results.

✓ Adjust **Zoom video and audio settings** to match your needs.

✓ Use **noise suppression and echo cancellation** to eliminate distractions.

✓ **Test your setup** before live presentations to avoid technical issues.

By implementing these strategies, you can **deliver compelling, clear, and engaging presentations** on Zoom every time!

3.3 Chat, Reactions, and Polling

3.3.1 Sending Messages in Chat

Introduction to Zoom Chat

The chat feature in Zoom is an essential communication tool that allows participants to send text messages during a meeting. It enhances interaction by enabling real-time messaging, private conversations, and group discussions without interrupting the speaker. Whether you need to share links, send files, or ask questions, Zoom's chat function provides a convenient way to stay engaged.

In this section, we will explore how to use the chat feature effectively, covering everything from sending basic messages to managing chat settings and security considerations.

1. Understanding Zoom Chat Options

Zoom chat offers several communication options during a meeting, allowing users to interact in different ways:

- **Public Messages**: Messages that everyone in the meeting can see.

- **Private Messages**: Messages sent directly to a specific participant, visible only to them.

- **File Sharing**: Sharing documents, images, and other files through the chat.

- **Emojis and Reactions in Chat**: Enhancing messages with emojis for better engagement.

- **Saved Chat Transcripts**: Downloading and saving chat history for future reference.

Before using the chat feature, it is important to understand these options to maximize your communication efficiency during a Zoom meeting.

2. How to Send a Message in Zoom Chat

2.1 Accessing the Chat Panel

To send a message in a Zoom meeting, follow these steps:

1. **Join or start a Zoom meeting.**

2. **Locate the chat icon** at the bottom of the Zoom meeting window. The icon looks like a speech bubble.

3. Click on **"Chat"** to open the chat panel. A sidebar or pop-up window will appear on the right side of your screen.

If you are using Zoom on a mobile device:

1. Tap the **"More"** option (three dots).

2. Select **"Chat"** to open the chat panel.

2.2 Sending a Public Message

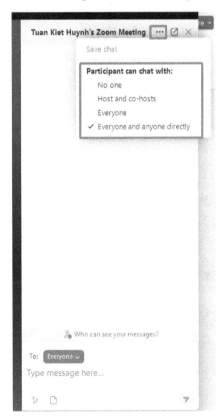

A public message is visible to everyone in the meeting. Here's how you can send one:

1. In the chat panel, locate the **"To"** field.

2. Select **"Everyone"** from the drop-down list.

3. Type your message in the text box.

4. Press **Enter (Return)** on your keyboard (or tap the send button on mobile) to send the message.

Once sent, your message will be displayed to all participants in the meeting.

2.3 Sending a Private Message

Private messages are useful when you need to communicate with a specific participant without disturbing the entire meeting.

1. Open the chat panel and click on the **"To"** field.

2. From the drop-down list, select the name of the participant you want to message.

3. Type your message in the text box.

4. Press **Enter (Return)** or tap the send button.

Private messages will only be visible to the selected participant, and they cannot be seen by the host or other attendees.

Note: In some meetings, the host may disable private messaging to prevent distractions.

2.4 Using Chat on Mobile Devices

On smartphones and tablets, the chat function works slightly differently:

1. Tap the **"More"** button (three dots) at the bottom-right corner of the screen.

2. Select **"Chat"** to open the chat panel.

3. Choose whether to send a message to **"Everyone"** or a specific person.

4. Type your message and tap **"Send."**

Although mobile chat is convenient, typing on a small screen can be slower compared to a computer, so consider keeping your messages concise.

3. Enhancing Communication with Chat Features

3.1 Sending Links and URLs

Zoom chat allows users to share website links with other participants. Simply copy and paste the link into the chat box, and Zoom will automatically format it as a clickable hyperlink.

Example:
☞ **https://zoom.us**

However, be mindful of security risks when clicking on unfamiliar links shared in the chat.

3.2 Attaching and Sending Files

If you need to share documents, PDFs, or images, Zoom allows file sharing through chat.

To send a file:

1. Open the chat panel.

2. Click the **File** icon (a paperclip symbol).

3. Select where to upload the file from (Your Computer, Google Drive, Dropbox, etc.).

4. Choose the file and click **"Send."**

On mobile, file-sharing options may be limited depending on the device and Zoom version.

3.3 Using Emojis and GIFs in Chat

To add a visual element to your messages, you can use emojis:

1. Click the **emoji icon** in the chat box.

2. Select an emoji and insert it into your message.

3. Press **Enter** to send.

Emojis help convey emotions and add personality to your communication. However, they should be used professionally in formal meetings.

4. Managing and Moderating Chat

4.1 Muting or Restricting Chat Messages

Meeting hosts have the ability to manage chat permissions to control distractions.

To restrict chat:

1. Click **"More"** in the chat panel.

2. Select **"Chat Settings."**

3. Choose from the following options:

   o **No one** (Disable chat completely).

   o **Host and Co-host only** (Only hosts can send messages).

   o **Everyone publicly** (Allow only public messages).

   o **Everyone publicly and privately** (Allow full messaging).

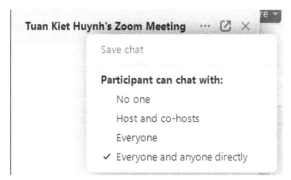

Restricting chat is useful in webinars where open discussions may not be needed.

4.2 Deleting a Message in Chat

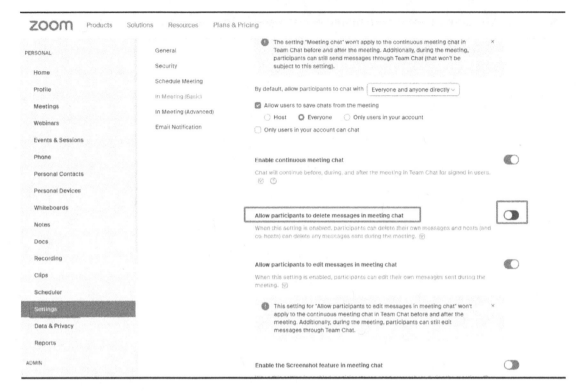

If you send a message by mistake, you can delete it before others see it:

1. Hover over the message.

2. Click the **three-dot menu** and select **"Delete."**

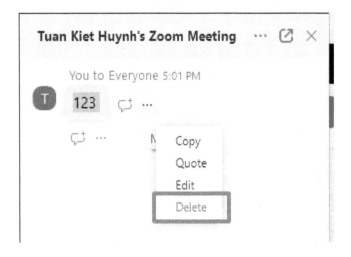

Note that hosts may have different deletion rights compared to participants.

---

5. Security and Privacy Considerations in Zoom Chat

To ensure a safe chat experience, follow these security best practices:

- Avoid sharing sensitive information like passwords or personal data.
- Be cautious of phishing attempts—never click on suspicious links.
- Hosts should moderate chat activity to prevent inappropriate messages.

Additionally, Zoom chat can be encrypted for privacy, ensuring that conversations remain secure.

Conclusion

The Zoom chat feature is a powerful tool that enhances communication and collaboration during meetings. By understanding how to send messages, share files, and manage chat settings, users can improve engagement and efficiency.

Mastering these chat functions will help you interact more effectively in Zoom meetings, whether for business, education, or personal use.

Next, we will explore how to use reactions and polling to further enhance interaction in Zoom meetings.

3.3.2 Using Emojis and Reactions

Introduction

In a virtual meeting environment, maintaining engagement and interaction is often a challenge. Zoom offers a variety of tools to help participants express themselves without disrupting the flow of the meeting. Among these tools, **emojis and reactions** play a crucial role in improving communication, fostering engagement, and creating a more interactive experience.

In this section, we will explore the different types of reactions available in Zoom, how to use them effectively, and best practices for making the most of these features in various meeting scenarios.

Understanding Zoom Reactions and Emojis

Before diving into how to use them, it's important to understand the different types of visual responses available in Zoom:

1. **Reactions (Non-Verbal Feedback):**

    o These are temporary visual indicators that appear on the screen or in the participant list.

    o Examples include 👍 (thumbs up), 👏 (clap), ❤️ (heart), 🚀 (rocket), etc.

    o They disappear after a few seconds or can be manually removed.

2. **Emojis (Chat-Based Reactions):**

    o Participants can send emojis through the Zoom chat, similar to how they function in messaging apps.

    o These remain in the chat window and do not disappear unless manually cleared.

3. **Raise Hand Feature:**

    o While not a traditional emoji or reaction, raising a hand is a crucial visual cue that allows participants to indicate that they want to speak.

    o It stays visible until the participant or host lowers it.

Each of these features serves a distinct purpose and can be used in different contexts to improve meeting efficiency and interaction.

How to Use Reactions in Zoom

1. Enabling Reactions

Before using reactions, make sure they are enabled in your Zoom settings.

For Participants:

1. Click on the **"Reactions"** button at the bottom of the Zoom meeting window.

2. Select the desired reaction (👋, 🖐, 🎉, etc.).

3. The reaction appears on the screen for a few seconds and then disappears.

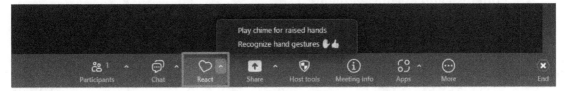

For Hosts:

1. Click **"Reactions"** on the toolbar.

2. Manage reaction settings by going to **Zoom Settings > Meeting > Reactions**.

3. Enable or disable specific reactions as needed.

💡 *Tip:* If reactions are not available, the host may have disabled them in the meeting settings.

---

2. Using Reactions Effectively

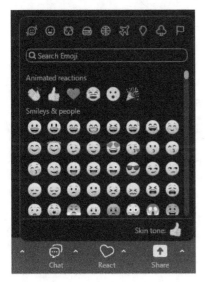

Reactions can be helpful in many meeting situations. Here are a few examples:

- **Voting and Quick Feedback:**

    o Instead of conducting a full poll, you can ask participants to react with a thumbs-up (👍) for agreement or a thumbs-down (👎) for disagreement.

- **Applause and Encouragement:**

    o Use the **clap reaction (👏)** to show appreciation for a speaker.

- **Emphasizing Key Points:**

    o The **heart (❤️)** or **party popper (🎉)** reaction can be used to celebrate milestones or positive moments.

- **Managing Large Meetings:**

    o In webinars or large meetings, reactions help participants provide quick feedback without interrupting the speaker.

💡 *Tip:* Encourage participants to use reactions as a form of non-verbal communication to keep the discussion flowing smoothly.

Using Emojis in Zoom Chat

1. How to Send Emojis in Zoom Chat

1. Open the **Chat** panel by clicking on **"Chat"** in the toolbar.

2. Click the **emoji icon (🙂)** in the chat box.

3. Choose an emoji from the menu or type emoji codes (e.g., :smile:).

4. Press **Enter** to send the emoji in chat.

💡 *Tip:* Some emojis can be entered using standard keyboard shortcuts, such as :) for ☺ or :(for ☹.

---

2. Best Practices for Using Emojis in Chat

Using emojis effectively in chat depends on the formality and purpose of the meeting. Here are some best practices:

✅ For Casual or Team Meetings:

- Emojis help express emotions and add personality to messages.
- Example: "Great job on that presentation! 🎉👏"

✅ For Business or Formal Meetings:

- Use emojis sparingly to maintain professionalism.
- Stick to simple expressions like 👍 or ☺.

✅ For Webinars or Large Meetings:

- Use emojis to acknowledge messages without cluttering the chat.
- Example: "Thanks for your question! ☺"

💡 *Tip:* If chat is disabled by the host, you won't be able to send emojis. Check with the host if you need chat access.

Customizing Reactions and Emojis

Zoom allows some customization of reactions and emojis to suit different preferences:

1. Changing Default Skin Tone for Reactions

- Click on **Zoom Settings > General**.
- Under **"Reactions"**, select your preferred skin tone.

2. Custom Emoji Support (For Chat)

- While Zoom doesn't currently support uploading custom emojis like Slack or Discord, you can use **Unicode emojis** from your keyboard.

💡 *Tip:* On Windows, use Win + . to open the emoji keyboard. On Mac, use Cmd + Ctrl + Space.

Advanced Tips and Tricks

1. Using Reactions in Breakout Rooms

- Reactions work inside breakout rooms, allowing small groups to provide feedback without disrupting the main session.

2. Using Emoji Reactions for Live Streaming

- If a Zoom meeting is live-streamed to platforms like YouTube or Facebook, reactions will appear in the stream, making them useful for audience engagement.

3. Combining Reactions and Polls

- While reactions provide instant feedback, they can be combined with **polls** for more detailed insights.

- Example: Use 👍 to gauge interest, then follow up with a poll for more detailed responses.

Common Issues and Troubleshooting

1. Reactions Are Not Showing

◆ Possible Causes:

- The host has disabled reactions.

- You are using an outdated Zoom version.

◆ Solution:

- Update Zoom to the latest version.

- Ask the host to enable reactions.

2. Emojis Not Appearing in Chat

◆ Possible Causes:

- Chat is disabled by the host.

- The Zoom app is experiencing a glitch.

◈ **Solution:**

- Check with the host to enable chat.

- Restart Zoom or update the app.

Conclusion

Emojis and reactions are small but powerful tools that can enhance the Zoom meeting experience. Whether used for quick feedback, engagement, or simply adding a bit of fun to a discussion, these features help create a more interactive virtual space.

Key Takeaways:

✅ Reactions provide instant, non-verbal feedback without disrupting the meeting.

✅ Emojis in chat add personality and emotion to written messages.

✅ Using these tools appropriately can improve meeting engagement and communication.

By understanding how and when to use emojis and reactions, you can make your Zoom meetings more dynamic and engaging for everyone involved.

3.3.3 Creating and Managing Polls

Polls are a powerful feature in Zoom that allows hosts to gather real-time feedback, conduct surveys, and enhance audience engagement during meetings. Whether you're running a business meeting, a training session, or an online class, polls help make interactions more dynamic and provide instant insights. In this section, we'll walk through everything you need to know about creating and managing polls in Zoom, including how to set them up, launch them during a meeting, and analyze the results.

Understanding Zoom Polls

Zoom's polling feature enables meeting hosts to create single-choice or multiple-choice questions that participants can answer in real time. These polls can be pre-created before the meeting starts or added during the meeting itself. Some key benefits of using polls include:

- **Gathering quick feedback** from participants.

- **Making meetings more interactive** by encouraging engagement.

- **Assessing audience understanding** in webinars and training sessions.

- **Voting on decisions** during business meetings or team discussions.

However, it's important to note that the polling feature is only available in scheduled meetings where the host has enabled it. Also, only licensed Zoom users can create and manage polls.

Enabling Polling in Zoom

Before you can create and launch polls, polling must be enabled in your Zoom settings. Follow these steps to activate polling:

1. **Sign in to Zoom Web Portal:**

   o Open a web browser and go to https://zoom.us/.

   o Sign in with your Zoom account credentials.

2. **Navigate to Polling Settings:**

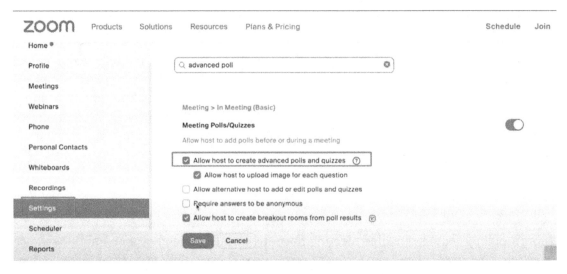

   o Click on **Settings** in the left-side menu.

   o Scroll down to the **Meeting (Advanced)** section.

    o Locate the **Polling** option and ensure it is turned **on**.

3. **Save Changes:**

    o If polling is disabled, toggle the switch to enable it.

    o Click **Save** to apply the changes.

Once polling is enabled, you can start creating polls for your meetings.

Creating a Poll Before a Meeting

Creating a poll before a meeting allows you to plan your questions in advance. Here's how you can set up a poll:

Step 1: Access Polls in Your Meeting Settings

- Go to the **Meetings** tab in your Zoom Web Portal.

- Click on the scheduled meeting for which you want to create a poll.

- Scroll down to find the **Polls/Quizzes** section.

Step 2: Create a New Poll

- Click **+ Create** to open the poll creation window.

- Enter a title for your poll.

- (Optional) Check **Enable quiz mode** if you want to set correct answers for each question.

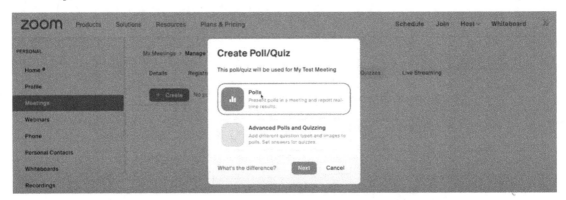

Step 3: Add Questions

- Click **Add a Question** to start creating poll questions.

- Choose the question type:

    ○ **Single Choice** (participants select one answer).

    ○ **Multiple Choice** (participants can select more than one answer).

- Type your question and provide answer choices.

- (Optional) If you enabled quiz mode, select the correct answer(s).

Untitled Poll

| Untitled Question | ☑ Multiple Choi... ⌄ |

Choice 1

Choice 2

+ Add Choice

🗑 ⧉

+ Add Question

Step 4: Save and Assign the Poll

- Click **Save** after adding all your questions.

- The poll will now be linked to your scheduled meeting and can be launched when needed.

Launching a Poll During a Meeting

Once your poll is created, you can launch it at any time during the meeting. Follow these steps:

Step 1: Open the Polling Tool

- Click on **Polls** in the meeting toolbar (only available if you are the host or co-host).

- Select the poll you want to launch from the list.

Step 2: Start the Poll

- Click **Launch Poll** to send it to participants.

- Participants will see the poll appear on their screen and can submit their responses.

Step 3: Monitor Poll Progress

- As participants respond, you can view real-time results.

- If needed, click **Re-launch Poll** to restart it for new responses.

Step 4: End the Poll and Share Results

- Click **End Poll** when you have received enough responses.

- Click **Share Results** if you want participants to see the poll outcomes.

Managing and Analyzing Poll Results

After the meeting, you can analyze poll results for further insights.

Viewing Poll Reports

- Go to the **Zoom Web Portal** and navigate to the **Reports** section.

- Select **Meeting** and click **Poll Report**.

- Choose the meeting for which you want to view poll results.

- Download the report as a CSV file.

Interpreting the Results

- Review the total number of participants who responded.

- Analyze the distribution of responses to gain insights.

- Use data to make informed decisions or improve future meetings.

Best Practices for Using Polls Effectively

To maximize the effectiveness of polls in Zoom meetings, consider these best practices:

1. Keep Polls Simple and Relevant

- Ensure questions are clear and easy to understand.

- Avoid overly complex or technical wording.

2. Use Polls to Increase Engagement

- Ask questions that encourage active participation.
- Use polls to check audience understanding or preferences.

3. Time Polls Strategically

- Introduce polls at key moments in the meeting.
- Allow enough time for participants to respond.

4. Combine Polls with Other Engagement Tools

- Follow up with a discussion after collecting responses.
- Use chat, reactions, or Q&A alongside polls for a richer experience.

5. Analyze Poll Results for Continuous Improvement

- Use feedback from polls to enhance future meetings.
- Adapt content and delivery based on participant responses.

Troubleshooting Common Polling Issues

Despite being a user-friendly feature, polling in Zoom may sometimes encounter issues. Below are common problems and their solutions:

1. Polls Option Not Available

- Ensure polling is enabled in **Zoom Web Settings**.
- Confirm you are the **host** (polls are not available to participants).

2. Participants Can't See the Poll

- Make sure the poll has been launched.
- Check if participants are using an updated Zoom version.

3. Poll Responses Not Being Collected

- Ask participants to submit their answers before closing the poll.
- If re-launching the poll, remind participants to answer again.

4. Unable to Download Poll Reports

- Check if the meeting was recorded, as some reports require recording.

- Ensure you have **admin permissions** to access reports.

Conclusion

Polling is an excellent tool for making Zoom meetings more interactive, engaging, and productive. Whether you're gathering quick feedback, facilitating decision-making, or enhancing training sessions, polls can significantly improve the meeting experience. By following best practices and troubleshooting common issues, you can leverage Zoom polls effectively to create dynamic and engaging virtual meetings.

Now that you understand how to create, launch, and manage polls, try implementing them in your next Zoom meeting to see the benefits firsthand!

CHAPTER IV
Advanced Zoom Features

4.1 Breakout Rooms for Group Discussions

4.1.1 Setting Up Breakout Rooms

Breakout Rooms are one of the most powerful features in Zoom, allowing hosts to divide participants into smaller groups for focused discussions, collaborative work, or team-building activities. This feature is widely used in business meetings, virtual classrooms, and online workshops to enhance engagement and productivity.

In this section, we will walk through the process of setting up Breakout Rooms, from enabling the feature to customizing and managing breakout sessions effectively.

1. Understanding Breakout Rooms in Zoom

Breakout Rooms function as separate, smaller Zoom sessions within the main meeting. Participants in these rooms can have their own discussions, share screens, and collaborate without disturbing the main meeting. The host can switch between rooms, send messages to all rooms, and bring participants back to the main session when needed.

Key Benefits of Breakout Rooms

- **Enhanced Collaboration**: Small groups allow for more focused discussions.

- **Better Engagement**: Participants are more likely to contribute in smaller groups.

- **Efficient Time Management**: Tasks and discussions can be divided among groups to cover more ground.

- **Customizable Experience**: Hosts can manually or automatically assign participants, set time limits, and configure settings to suit the meeting's goals.

2. Enabling Breakout Rooms in Zoom

Before using Breakout Rooms in a meeting, the feature must be enabled in the Zoom settings.

Step 1: Accessing Zoom Settings

1. Sign in to your Zoom account at https://zoom.us.

2. Click on **Settings** in the left-hand menu.

3. Navigate to the **Meeting** tab.

4. Scroll down to the **In Meeting (Advanced)** section.

5. Locate **Breakout Room** and ensure the toggle switch is turned ON.

Step 2: Configuring Breakout Room Options

Once enabled, you have the following options:

- **Allow host to assign participants to breakout rooms when scheduling** – If checked, hosts can pre-assign participants before the meeting starts.

- **Allow participants to choose their own room** – If enabled, participants can join rooms of their choice instead of being assigned by the host.

3. Creating and Managing Breakout Rooms During a Meeting

Once Breakout Rooms are enabled in your account settings, you can create and manage them during an active Zoom meeting.

Step 1: Opening the Breakout Rooms Panel

1. Start a Zoom meeting as the host.

2. Click on the **Breakout Rooms** button in the meeting toolbar.

3. A new window will appear, allowing you to create and assign rooms.

Step 2: Choosing the Number of Rooms

Zoom allows you to create up to **100** Breakout Rooms, depending on your Zoom plan.

1. In the Breakout Rooms window, choose the number of rooms needed.

2. Assign participants using one of the following methods:

   o **Automatically**: Zoom will distribute participants equally among rooms.

   o **Manually**: The host assigns each participant to a specific room.

   o **Let participants choose**: Participants can select which room to join.

Step 3: Assigning Participants to Rooms

If you select **Manual Assignment**, follow these steps:

1. Click **Assign** next to each Breakout Room.

2. Select participants from the list.

3. Click **Open All Rooms** to start the session.

For **pre-assigned rooms**, you can upload a CSV file with participant details in the Zoom web portal.

4. Customizing Breakout Room Settings

Adjusting Room Features

Before opening Breakout Rooms, the host can customize various settings:

- **Allow participants to return to the main session at any time** – Participants can leave their room and return to the main meeting freely.

- **Auto-close breakout rooms after X minutes** – The rooms will close automatically after a set duration.

- **Countdown timer** – A timer will notify participants before rooms close.

Broadcasting Messages to Breakout Rooms

Hosts can send messages to all Breakout Rooms to provide instructions or updates.

1. Click **Breakout Rooms** > **Broadcast a message to all**.

2. Type your message and click **Broadcast**.

3. The message will appear in all rooms.

5. Managing Breakout Rooms During a Session

Joining and Leaving Breakout Rooms

Hosts can move between Breakout Rooms to monitor discussions and provide guidance:

1. Click **Breakout Rooms** in the toolbar.

2. Select the room you want to join.

3. Click **Join** and enter the room.

Closing Breakout Rooms

When it's time to bring everyone back:

1. Click **Close All Rooms**.

2. Participants will see a **60-second countdown timer** before returning to the main session.

6. Best Practices for Using Breakout Rooms

✅ Plan Ahead

- Prepare clear discussion topics or tasks before assigning participants.
- Set time limits to keep discussions on track.

✅ Provide Instructions

- Use the **Broadcast Message** feature to guide participants.
- Assign a facilitator in each room to keep the conversation focused.

✅ Encourage Participation

- Ask open-ended questions to spark discussions.
- Rotate speakers to ensure everyone has a chance to contribute.

7. Common Issues and Troubleshooting

Issue 1: Participants Can't Join Breakout Rooms

Solution: Ensure Breakout Rooms are enabled in the host's Zoom settings.

Issue 2: Participants Are Assigned Incorrectly

Solution: Double-check assignments before opening the rooms or allow manual selection.

Issue 3: Breakout Rooms Won't Close

Solution: Click "Close All Rooms" again or manually remove participants from rooms.

Conclusion

Breakout Rooms are an essential tool for fostering collaboration, brainstorming ideas, and enhancing engagement in virtual meetings. By mastering the process of setting up and managing Breakout Rooms, hosts can create more productive and interactive online sessions. With proper planning and clear instructions, Breakout Rooms can transform any Zoom meeting into a highly effective experience.

4.1.2 Assigning Participants Manually vs. Automatically

Introduction to Assigning Participants in Breakout Rooms

Breakout rooms are a powerful feature in Zoom that allow meeting hosts to divide participants into smaller groups for discussions, collaboration, or activities. Once breakout rooms are created, participants must be assigned to these rooms. Zoom offers two primary ways to assign participants: **manual assignment** and **automatic assignment**. Understanding the differences between these methods and when to use each is crucial for ensuring an efficient and organized meeting experience.

In this section, we will explore the **manual and automatic assignment methods**, their advantages and limitations, and best practices for managing participant allocation in breakout rooms.

1. Overview of Assignment Methods

Zoom provides three options for assigning participants to breakout rooms:

1. **Manually assigning participants** – The host selects which participants go into each room.

2. **Automatically assigning participants** – Zoom randomly distributes participants into rooms.

3. **Letting participants choose a room** – Participants select their own rooms (available in newer Zoom versions).

We will focus on the first two methods—**manual and automatic assignment**—as they are the primary ways hosts can control breakout room allocation.

2. Automatic Assignment: The Quick and Easy Option

2.1 How Automatic Assignment Works

Automatic assignment allows the host to let Zoom distribute participants randomly into breakout rooms. This is the fastest method and is useful when:

- The meeting has a large number of participants.

- Participants do not need to be in specific groups.

- The host wants to save time by avoiding manual sorting.

2.2 Steps to Use Automatic Assignment

1. **Start a Zoom Meeting** – Ensure that you are the **host** or **co-host**.

2. **Open the Breakout Rooms Panel** – Click on the "Breakout Rooms" button in the Zoom toolbar.

3. **Choose the Number of Rooms** – Enter the number of breakout rooms needed.

4. **Select "Automatically" Assign Participants** – Zoom will evenly distribute participants across the rooms.

5. **Click "Create"** – The rooms will be generated, and participants will be assigned randomly.

6. **Start the Breakout Sessions** – Click "Open All Rooms" to begin.

2.3 Advantages of Automatic Assignment

✅ **Time-Saving** – Ideal for large meetings where manually assigning people would be inefficient.
✅ **Balanced Groups** – Ensures participants are evenly distributed.
✅ **Easy for the Host** – Reduces the need for pre-planning and manual sorting.

2.4 Limitations of Automatic Assignment

✖ **Lack of Control** – The host cannot decide which participants are grouped together.
✖ **Not Ideal for Teamwork** – If specific teams need to work together, automatic assignment   is   not   the   best   option.
✖ **Random Distribution** – Some participants may not be comfortable working with strangers.

---

3. Manual Assignment: More Control, More Effort

3.1 How Manual Assignment Works

Manual assignment allows the host to hand-pick which participants go into each room. This method is useful when:

- Participants need to be grouped based on **specific criteria** (e.g., teams, departments, or skill levels).

- The host wants to create a **customized experience** for each group.

- The meeting involves **structured activities** that require pre-defined groupings.

3.2 Steps to Manually Assign Participants

1. **Start a Zoom Meeting** – The host must have **breakout rooms enabled**.

2. **Open the Breakout Rooms Panel** – Click the "Breakout Rooms" button.

3. **Choose the Number of Rooms** – Decide how many rooms you need.

4. **Select "Manually" Assign Participants** – This will allow you to place each participant in a specific room.

5. **Assign Participants One by One** – Click each participant's name and assign them to a room.

6. **Adjust as Needed** – You can move participants between rooms before starting the session.

7. **Open the Breakout Sessions** – Click "Open All Rooms" when you are ready.

3.3 Advantages of Manual Assignment

✅ **Greater Control** – The host decides how participants are grouped.
✅ **Ideal for Team-Based Work** – Ensures that relevant people work together.
✅ **Better for Engagement** – Assigns participants based on shared interests or expertise.

3.4 Limitations of Manual Assignment

✖ **Time-Consuming** – Requires effort, especially for large meetings.
✖ **Not Suitable for Large Groups** – Manually sorting hundreds of participants is impractical.
✖ **Requires Pre-Planning** – The host must know in advance how to assign people.

4. Choosing the Right Assignment Method

The best assignment method depends on the **type of meeting and the desired outcome**. Below is a comparison to help decide:

Criteria	Manual Assignment	Automatic Assignment
Speed & Efficiency	Slower, requires effort	Faster, immediate assignment
Control Over Grouping	High – host chooses groups	Low – random distribution
Best for Large Meetings	No, too time-consuming	Yes, quick and effective
Best for Team-Based Work	Yes, ensures teams work together	No, teams may be split up
Flexibility	Can adjust assignments	Cannot adjust once assigned

When to Use Manual Assignment:

- Training sessions where participants need to be grouped based on expertise.

- Team-building exercises where pre-defined teams exist.

- Small meetings where specific discussions are required.

When to Use Automatic Assignment:

- Large webinars where quick group discussions are needed.

- Casual networking sessions where random interactions are beneficial.

- Time-sensitive meetings where setup must be quick.

5. Tips for Assigning Participants Effectively

Regardless of the method you choose, here are some **best practices**:

- **Use Pre-Assigned Breakout Rooms** – If you know participants' names in advance, you can assign them before the meeting starts.

- **Communicate Room Assignments Clearly** – Let participants know which room they are assigned to and why.

- **Monitor and Adjust** – Hosts can move participants if needed.

- **Balance Group Sizes** – Ensure each breakout room has a manageable number of participants.

- **Provide Instructions Before Assigning** – Participants should understand their objectives in breakout sessions.

Conclusion

Choosing between manual and automatic assignment in Zoom's breakout rooms depends on the specific needs of your meeting. Automatic assignment is perfect for quick and random grouping, whereas manual assignment gives hosts greater control over the organization and structure of breakout rooms.

Understanding the strengths and limitations of each method helps create efficient, engaging, and productive virtual meetings. By following best practices, hosts can ensure that breakout rooms serve their intended purpose—whether it's collaboration, networking, or learning.

4.1.3 Managing Breakout Sessions

Introduction to Managing Breakout Sessions

Breakout rooms are a powerful feature in Zoom that allows meeting hosts to split participants into smaller groups for focused discussions, team collaborations, or workshop-style activities. However, simply creating breakout rooms is not enough—effective management ensures smooth transitions, productive discussions, and an overall seamless experience for participants.

In this section, we will explore the key aspects of managing breakout sessions, including monitoring participants, communicating effectively, troubleshooting common issues, and optimizing breakout sessions for different meeting types.

1. Pre-Session Management: Setting the Stage

Preparing for Breakout Sessions

Before launching breakout rooms, it is essential to plan ahead to ensure they align with your meeting goals. Consider the following aspects:

- Define the Purpose: What do you want participants to achieve in their groups? Define clear objectives.

- Assign Facilitators: If possible, assign co-hosts or moderators to help guide discussions in breakout rooms.

- Determine the Number of Rooms: The number of breakout rooms should depend on the total number of participants and the nature of the discussion.

- Set a Time Limit: Specify how long the breakout sessions will last to keep discussions structured.

Choosing the Right Assignment Method

When setting up breakout rooms, you can assign participants in three ways:

- Manually: The host selects participants for each room. Ideal for controlled discussions.

- Automatically: Zoom distributes participants evenly across rooms. Best for quick and random grouping.

- Self-Selection: Participants choose which breakout room to join. Suitable for open discussions.

Tip: If your meeting requires specific expertise in each room, manually assign participants based on their background or role.

2. In-Session Management: Facilitating Engagement and Productivity

Once breakout rooms are active, the host has various tools to ensure a productive session.

Monitoring Breakout Rooms

As a host or co-host, you can monitor discussions in the breakout rooms to ensure they stay on track. Zoom provides these options:

- Joining Breakout Rooms: The host can move between rooms to check progress and assist participants.

- Asking Participants for Feedback: Encourage them to use the "Ask for Help" button if they need assistance.

- Broadcasting Messages: Send messages to all rooms to provide reminders or instructions.

Best Practice: If breakout rooms last longer than 10 minutes, visit each room briefly to ensure participants are engaged and understand their tasks.

Communicating with Participants

Clear communication is essential to guide participants through the breakout session. Utilize these methods:

- Text Announcements: Send important messages via the "Broadcast Message to All" feature.

- Pre-Assigned Discussion Questions: Share key discussion points before splitting participants into rooms.

- Co-Host Support: Assign co-hosts to specific rooms to facilitate conversation.

Example   message:
"You have 10 minutes left! Please summarize your discussion points before returning to the main session."

Managing Time Effectively

Time management is crucial for breakout sessions. Here's how to keep discussions on track:

- Use a Countdown Timer: When the session is about to end, participants will see a countdown before returning to the main room.

- Set Clear Time Limits: Inform participants of the session duration beforehand.

- Send Time Warnings: Regularly update participants on how much time remains.

Pro Tip: If a discussion requires more time, you can extend the session duration from the breakout room settings.

---

3. Troubleshooting Common Issues

Even well-planned breakout sessions may encounter issues. Here's how to address common problems:

Participants Having Trouble Joining

Some participants may have difficulty entering breakout rooms due to:

- Older Zoom versions: Ask participants to update their Zoom client.

- Connection issues: Recommend reconnecting or joining via another device.

- Mobile limitations: Some breakout room features may not work on mobile devices.

Solution: If a participant is unable to join, manually assign them to a room from the main session.

Participants Needing Help Inside Breakout Rooms

If participants require assistance, they can click the "Ask for Help" button. The host will receive a notification and can join the room to assist.

Alternative Solution: Use the chat function to answer simple questions without entering the breakout room.

Participants Accidentally Leaving the Breakout Room

If someone accidentally leaves, they may need to be reassigned. The host can do this by:

1. Opening the Breakout Rooms panel

2. Locating the participant

3. Assigning them to the correct room

No One Talking in the Breakout Room

Some groups may struggle to start discussions. To encourage engagement:

- Assign a leader to facilitate discussions

- Provide structured discussion questions

- Encourage all participants to contribute

4. Post-Session Management: Wrapping Up Effectively

Bringing Participants Back to the Main Room

When the breakout session ends, all participants return to the main meeting room. The host can:

- Use the Automatic Timer to close rooms when the session time is up.
- Manually Close All Rooms from the Zoom control panel.

Best Practice: Give participants a 30-second warning before ending the session to avoid abrupt transitions.

Debriefing and Summarizing Discussions

After the breakout session, encourage participants to:

- Share key takeaways from their group discussions.
- Assign a representative from each room to summarize findings.
- Use the Zoom chat feature to collect feedback.

Gathering Participant Feedback

To improve future sessions, gather feedback by:

- Asking participants to rate the breakout experience in chat.
- Using Zoom's polling feature to collect responses.
- Sending a post-meeting survey via email.

Example questions:

- Did you find the breakout room discussions helpful?
- What could be improved in future sessions?

Conclusion

Managing breakout sessions effectively is key to fostering engagement and collaboration in Zoom meetings. By preparing ahead, monitoring discussions, troubleshooting issues, and ensuring a smooth wrap-up, you can maximize the value of breakout rooms for your participants.

By applying these strategies, you can turn Zoom breakout rooms into a dynamic tool for learning, brainstorming, and team collaboration. Whether you're hosting business meetings, training workshops, or educational sessions, mastering breakout room management will enhance the overall effectiveness of your Zoom meetings.

4.2 Recording and Transcription

4.2.1 How to Record a Meeting

Recording a Zoom meeting is an essential feature for individuals and organizations that need to keep track of important discussions, presentations, training sessions, or virtual events. Zoom provides two main recording options: **local recording**, which saves the file to your device, and **cloud recording**, which stores the file on Zoom's cloud servers (available only for paid accounts). This section will guide you through the entire process of recording a Zoom meeting, including setup, permissions, recording controls, and best practices.

1. Understanding Zoom Recording Options

Local Recording vs. Cloud Recording

Before you start recording, it's important to understand the differences between the two available options:

Feature	Local Recording	Cloud Recording (Paid Plans Only)
Storage Location	Saved on your computer	Stored in Zoom's cloud servers
Access	Only accessible from the device where recorded	Accessible from any device via a Zoom account
File Formats	MP4 (video), M4A (audio), TXT (transcription if enabled)	MP4, M4A, TXT, and other formats
Transcription	Not available by default	Automatic transcription available
Sharing Options	Must be manually uploaded to a sharing platform	Can be shared via a Zoom-generated link

Who Can Record a Zoom Meeting?

By default, only the meeting host has permission to record a Zoom session. However, the host can grant recording privileges to participants. This is particularly useful for collaborative meetings, training sessions, or webinars where multiple people may need to record the session.

- Hosts and Co-Hosts: Automatically have permission to record.

- Participants: Can record only if the host grants permission.

2. Setting Up and Enabling Recording

2.1 Enabling Local Recording

To enable local recording, follow these steps:

For Individual Users:

1. Sign in to your **Zoom account** at https://zoom.us.

2. Click on your **profile picture** and go to **Settings**.

3. Navigate to the **Recording** tab.

4. Under **Local Recording**, toggle the switch to enable it.

For Admins (Business & Enterprise Accounts):

1. Sign in to the **Zoom Admin Portal**.

2. Go to **Account Settings**.

3. Under **Recording**, ensure **Local Recording** is enabled for all users.

2.2 Enabling Cloud Recording (For Paid Plans)

If you have a **Zoom Pro, Business, or Enterprise account**, you can enable cloud recording:

1. Go to **Zoom Account Settings**.

2. Click on the **Recording** tab.

3. Toggle the switch for **Cloud Recording**.

4. Adjust settings such as recording audio transcripts and recording active speaker or gallery view.

3. Recording a Zoom Meeting

3.1 Starting a Local Recording

Once the recording feature is enabled, follow these steps to start recording:

1. **Start or join** a Zoom meeting.

2. **Click on the "Record" button** at the bottom of the meeting window.

3. Choose **"Record on this Computer"** (for local recording).

4. A recording indicator will appear on the top-left of the screen.

5. To **pause or stop recording**, click on the "Pause/Stop Recording" button.

6. Once the meeting ends, Zoom will automatically convert the recording to an **MP4 file**, which will be saved in your **default Zoom folder** (usually in "Documents > Zoom").

3.2 Starting a Cloud Recording (Paid Users Only)

If you are using a paid Zoom plan, you can record to the cloud:

1. **Start or join** a Zoom meeting.

2. Click **"Record"** and select **"Record to the Cloud"**.

3. The recording will automatically be saved to your **Zoom account** and can be accessed later at **zoom.us/recordings**.

4. You will receive an **email notification** once the recording is processed and ready for download or sharing.

3.3 Granting Recording Permission to Participants

If you want another participant to record the meeting, follow these steps:

1. Click on **Participants** in the Zoom toolbar.

2. Find the participant's name and click **More**.

3. Select **"Allow to Record"**.

4. The participant will receive a notification confirming their recording permissions.

4. Managing and Accessing Zoom Recordings

4.1 Finding Your Local Recordings

By default, local recordings are stored in the following locations:

- **Windows:** C:\Users\[Your Username]\Documents\Zoom

- **Mac:** /Users/[Your Username]/Documents/Zoom

To manually find a recording:

1. Open the **Zoom app**.

2. Click **Meetings** > **Recorded**.

3. Select the meeting recording you want to access.

4.2 Accessing Cloud Recordings

To access cloud recordings:

1. Log in to your **Zoom web portal**.

2. Click **Recordings** on the left panel.

3. Find your recorded meeting and click **Download**, **Share**, or **Delete**.

4.3 Sharing a Zoom Recording

You can share a Zoom recording by:

- **Uploading local recordings** to Google Drive, Dropbox, or YouTube.

- **Sharing a cloud recording link** (Zoom provides a direct shareable link).

5. Best Practices for Recording Zoom Meetings

Inform Participants Before Recording

- Always ask for consent before recording, especially in professional settings.
- Use Zoom's "Recording Disclaimer" feature to notify participants when recording starts.

Optimize Video and Audio Quality

- Use a good microphone for clearer audio.
- Adjust lighting to enhance video clarity.
- Close unnecessary applications to avoid performance issues.

Manage Cloud Storage Wisely

- Regularly delete old recordings to free up space.
- Download and backup important recordings to external drives.

Enable Automatic Transcription (For Cloud Recording)

- Helps create meeting summaries and make content searchable.
- Available under Recording Settings > "Enable Audio Transcription".

6. Troubleshooting Common Recording Issues

Recording Button Not Showing Up

- Ensure recording is enabled in Zoom settings.
- Confirm you have the necessary permissions.

Poor Audio/Video Quality in Recordings

- Use a wired internet connection for stability.
- Adjust Zoom video settings for higher resolution recording.

Recording Storage Issues

- Free up space on your hard drive or cloud storage.
- Change the default recording location in Zoom settings.

Conclusion

Recording Zoom meetings is an invaluable tool for businesses, educators, and professionals. By understanding the differences between local and cloud recording, setting up recording permissions, and applying best practices, you can ensure that your recordings are **clear, accessible, and secure**.

4.2.2 Local vs. Cloud Recording

Introduction

Recording Zoom meetings is an essential feature for businesses, educators, and individuals who want to keep track of discussions, share sessions with others, or review content later. Zoom provides two main recording options: Local Recording and Cloud Recording. Understanding the differences between these two options will help you choose the best one based on your needs, storage capacity, and access preferences.

This section will explore the key differences between local and cloud recording, their advantages and limitations, and provide step-by-step instructions for using both effectively.

1. Overview of Local and Cloud Recording

Zoom offers **two types of recordings**, each with its own functionalities and storage options:

Feature	Local Recording	Cloud Recording
Storage Location	Stored on the user's computer (hard drive)	Stored on Zoom's cloud servers
Availability	Available for all Zoom accounts (including free users)	Available only for **paid plans** (Pro, Business, Enterprise, and Education)
Accessibility	Can only be accessed on the device where it was recorded (unless manually uploaded)	Can be accessed from any device with an internet connection

Storage Limit	Limited by the user's local disk space	Limited by the cloud storage quota of the Zoom plan
Backup & Security	User is responsible for backing up files	Zoom provides cloud security and backup options
Sharing Options	Must manually upload to platforms like Google Drive, Dropbox, or YouTube	Direct sharing via a link with security settings

Now, let's explore each type of recording in detail.

2. Local Recording: How It Works

What Is Local Recording?

Local recording allows you to save Zoom meetings directly to your computer's hard drive. This feature is available for both free and paid Zoom accounts. Once a meeting is recorded, the files are saved in MP4 (video), M4A (audio), and TXT (chat) formats.

Advantages of Local Recording

✅ Available for all Zoom users (no need for a paid plan)
✅ No storage limits (other than your computer's storage capacity)
✅ Faster access to files without internet dependency
✅ More control over editing and uploading the video

Limitations of Local Recording

✖ Not accessible on multiple devices (unless manually uploaded)
✖ Risk of data loss if your computer crashes or runs out of space
✖ Manual sharing required to distribute the recording

How to Enable and Use Local Recording

Step 1: Enable Local Recording in Zoom Settings

1. **Sign in** to the Zoom web portal (https://zoom.us).

2. Click on **Settings** in the left panel.

3. Under the **Recording** tab, toggle **Local Recording** ON.

Step 2: Record a Meeting Locally

1. Start a **Zoom meeting** as the **host**.

2. Click the **Record** button in the Zoom toolbar.

3. Choose **"Record on this Computer."**

4. Zoom will begin recording, and a small indicator will appear.

Step 3: Find and Manage Your Recordings

- Once the meeting ends, Zoom will **convert the recording** into an MP4 file.

- By default, the file is saved in:

   - **Windows:** C:\Users\YourName\Documents\Zoom

   - **Mac:** /Users/YourName/Documents/Zoom

- You can manually upload the file to **Google Drive, Dropbox, or YouTube** for easy access.

---

3. Cloud Recording: How It Works

What Is Cloud Recording?

Cloud recording allows you to store Zoom meetings on Zoom's servers instead of saving them locally. This feature is **only available for paid Zoom accounts** (Pro, Business, Enterprise, and Education).

Advantages of Cloud Recording

✓ Access from anywhere via the Zoom web portal
✓ Automatic backup and security (reduces the risk of losing files)
✓ Direct sharing with a link (no need to manually upload the file)
✓ Additional recording options, such as recording separate audio tracks for each participant

Limitations of Cloud Recording

✘ Only available for paid users

✘ Storage limits depend on your Zoom plan

✘ Requires an internet connection to access recordings

3.4 How to Enable and Use Cloud Recording

Step 1: Enable Cloud Recording in Zoom Settings

1. Sign in to the **Zoom web portal**.

2. Go to **Settings > Recording**.

3. Toggle **Cloud Recording** ON.

Step 2: Record a Meeting to the Cloud

1. Start a **Zoom meeting** as the **host**.

2. Click **Record > Record to the Cloud**.

3. A message will appear indicating that **the meeting is being recorded to Zoom's cloud**.

Step 3: Access and Manage Your Cloud Recordings

*   Sign in to **Zoom's web portal** and go to **Recordings**.

*   Download, delete, or share recordings **directly from the cloud**.

4. Choosing Between Local and Cloud Recording

When to Use Local Recording

Use local recording if:

✔ You don't have a paid Zoom account

✔ You need unlimited storage (limited only by your computer's space)

✔ You prefer manual control over file management and editing

When to Use Cloud Recording

Use cloud recording if:

✔ You need to access recordings from any device

✓ You want automatic backups and security

✓ You want to share recordings easily with a link

---

5. Best Practices for Zoom Recording

Before the Meeting

✓ Ensure your Zoom settings allow the correct recording type.

✓ Check your microphone, camera, and internet stability.

✓ Notify participants that the meeting is being recorded (for legal and ethical reasons).

During the Meeting

✓ Start recording early to avoid missing any content.

✓ Use mute/unmute controls to avoid unwanted noise.

✓ If using cloud recording, ensure you have enough storage space.

After the Meeting

✓ Save and organize your local recordings properly.

✓ If using cloud recording, delete old files to free up space.

✓ Edit and share the recording as needed.

---

6. Conclusion

Both local and cloud recording offer valuable benefits, but choosing the right one depends on your needs. Local recording is great for users who prefer to store files on their own devices, while cloud recording is ideal for those who need remote access, automatic backups, and easy sharing.

By understanding how to use both local and cloud recording effectively, you can ensure that your Zoom meetings are recorded safely, stored securely, and shared efficiently.

Ready to record your next Zoom meeting? Choose the right method and start capturing important conversations today!

✓ **Key Takeaways:**

✓ **Local Recording:** Best for users who need offline storage and control.
✓ **Cloud Recording:** Best for businesses and educators who need remote access and easy sharing.
✓ **Best Practices:** Always check settings before recording, ensure enough storage, and notify participants.

4.2.3 Using Live Transcription and Subtitles

Introduction to Live Transcription and Subtitles

Live transcription and subtitles in Zoom are powerful accessibility features that enhance the meeting experience for a diverse audience. These tools provide real-time captions for spoken dialogue, making it easier for participants who are hard of hearing, non-native speakers, or those in noisy environments to follow the conversation.

In this section, we will explore how to enable live transcription, customize subtitle settings, and use third-party integrations to enhance accessibility in Zoom meetings.

Understanding Live Transcription in Zoom

Live transcription is an automated feature that uses speech-to-text technology to provide captions in real-time. This feature is available for Zoom users on Pro, Business, Enterprise, and Education accounts.

How Live Transcription Works

- Zoom's AI-driven system listens to the meeting audio and converts it into text.

- The transcription appears at the bottom of the screen as captions.

- The accuracy of the transcription depends on factors such as speaker clarity, background noise, and audio quality.

Who Benefits from Live Transcription?

- Hearing-impaired participants – Ensures accessibility for individuals with hearing difficulties.

- Non-native speakers – Helps people understand spoken content more clearly.

- Participants in noisy environments – Allows attendees to follow conversations without relying solely on audio.

- Students and professionals – Aids note-taking and improves information retention.

Enabling and Managing Live Transcription

Live transcription must be enabled by the meeting host or co-host before participants can access it.

Step 1: Enabling Live Transcription in Zoom Settings

Before using live transcription, ensure it is enabled in your Zoom settings:

1. **Sign in** to your Zoom account at Zoom.us.

2. **Go to Settings** and select the **Meeting** tab.

3. Scroll down to **In Meeting (Advanced)** and locate **Automated Captions**.

4. **Toggle on** the option for **Live Transcription**.

5. If you want to allow meeting participants to request live transcription, check the box for **Allow participants to request live transcription**.

Step 2: Enabling Live Transcription During a Meeting

Once the setting is enabled, the host can turn on live transcription during a meeting:

1. **Start a Zoom meeting** as the host.

2. Click on the **Live Transcript** button in the meeting toolbar.

3. Select **Enable Auto-Transcription**.

4. Participants will now see captions at the bottom of their screen.

Step 3: Managing Live Transcription Options

Once enabled, the host can manage transcription settings:

- **View Full Transcript** – Allows participants to open a side panel with the full transcript history.

- **Save Transcript** – Hosts can enable or disable this option.

- **Disable Transcription** – Hosts can turn off live transcription at any time.

4.2.3.3 Customizing Subtitles in Zoom

Participants can personalize subtitle settings for better readability.

Adjusting Subtitle Size

To change the subtitle size:

1. Click on the **Live Transcript** button.

2. Select **Subtitle Settings**.

3. Adjust the **Font Size** slider to make text larger or smaller.

Hiding and Showing Subtitles

- If subtitles are distracting, participants can click **Hide Subtitle** to remove them.

- To restore subtitles, click **Show Subtitle** from the transcript menu.

Translating Captions in Zoom

Zoom now offers **Live Translation** as a paid add-on for certain accounts. This feature automatically translates captions into multiple languages, enhancing accessibility for international meetings.

Using Third-Party Captioning Services

For improved accuracy and additional language options, third-party captioning services can be integrated with Zoom.

Popular Third-Party Captioning Tools

- **Otter.ai** – Offers live captions and post-meeting transcription.
- **Rev Live Captions** – Provides professional-quality captions in real time.
- **Verbit** – Uses AI-powered and human-reviewed transcriptions for high accuracy.

How to Enable Third-Party Captions in Zoom

1. In **Zoom Settings**, go to **Meeting (Advanced)**.
2. Enable **Manual Captioning** and **Allow use of third-party captioning services**.
3. Share the **API Token** with your captioning service provider.
4. Start a meeting and activate captions from the third-party tool.

Recording and Saving Transcriptions

Zoom allows meeting hosts to save transcriptions for future reference.

How to Save Live Transcription

1. Click on the **Live Transcript** button.
2. Select **Save Transcript**.
3. The file will be saved as a **.txt** document in your Zoom folder.

Recording a Meeting with Captions

If you want to record a Zoom meeting with subtitles:

1. **Start a Cloud Recording** (Local recordings do not save captions).

2. Ensure **Live Transcription** is enabled.

3. After the meeting, access the **Zoom Cloud Recordings** to download the video with embedded captions.

Best Practices for Using Live Transcription

To improve transcription accuracy and ensure an optimal experience, follow these best practices:

1. Speak Clearly and Slowly

- Avoid speaking too fast to allow the AI to process words correctly.

- Enunciate words clearly to reduce errors.

2. Use High-Quality Audio Equipment

- A good microphone reduces background noise and improves speech recognition.

- Encourage participants to mute their microphones when not speaking.

3. Minimize Background Noise

- Conduct meetings in a quiet space.

- Use noise-canceling software or Zoom's **Noise Suppression** feature.

4. Assign a Live Captioner if Needed

- For important meetings, consider using a **manual captioner** to improve accuracy.

5. Inform Participants About Transcriptions

- Let attendees know if transcriptions are being recorded to maintain transparency.

Conclusion

Live transcription and subtitles are essential tools that enhance accessibility and engagement in Zoom meetings. By enabling and customizing these features, hosts can ensure a more inclusive experience for all participants. Additionally, third-party services and cloud recording options offer further flexibility for those who require high-quality captions.

By following the best practices outlined in this section, you can maximize the effectiveness of Zoom's live transcription feature and ensure smooth communication in your virtual meetings.

4.3 Security and Privacy Settings

4.3.1 Enabling End-to-End Encryption

Introduction

In today's digital landscape, security and privacy have become paramount, especially in online communication platforms like Zoom. With the rise of remote work, virtual classrooms, and online events, ensuring that conversations remain private and secure is crucial. One of the most advanced security features Zoom offers is End-to-End Encryption (E2EE).

This section will explore what E2EE is, how it enhances security, the differences between E2EE and Zoom's default encryption methods, and how to enable it for your meetings. We will also discuss the limitations of E2EE and provide best practices for ensuring secure Zoom communications.

What is End-to-End Encryption (E2EE)?

End-to-End Encryption (E2EE) is a security protocol that ensures only the participants of a meeting can decrypt and access the content of the conversation. This means that even Zoom itself cannot see or hear what is being shared in the meeting because the encryption keys are stored only on users' devices and not on Zoom's servers.

With E2EE enabled:
✅ Meeting data is encrypted on the sender's device and only decrypted on the recipient's device.
✅ No third party (including Zoom, internet service providers, or hackers) can intercept the communication.
✅ Only authorized participants in the meeting can access shared content.

How Does Zoom's E2EE Differ from Other Encryption Methods?

Zoom provides different levels of encryption for meetings:

1. Standard Encryption (AES-256 GCM) – Default Security

- Zoom meetings, by default, use **Advanced Encryption Standard (AES) 256-bit encryption** in Galois/Counter Mode (GCM).

- This provides strong security but still allows Zoom's servers to process the meeting (e.g., enabling cloud recording or live transcription).

- While this protects against external cyber threats, Zoom has access to the meeting data if necessary.

2. End-to-End Encryption (E2EE) – Maximum Privacy

- When E2EE is enabled, encryption keys are **generated and stored only on users' devices** instead of Zoom's servers.

- No one outside the meeting—including Zoom—can decrypt the conversation.

- Certain features, like cloud recording and live transcription, are disabled since Zoom's servers cannot access the meeting content.

Limitations of Using E2EE in Zoom

While E2EE provides **maximum security**, it comes with some **functional limitations**:

✘ Cloud Recording is Disabled – Since Zoom's servers cannot decrypt the meeting, cloud recording is not available. You can still use local recording on your computer.
✘ Live Transcription and Third-Party Services are Disabled – Features that rely on Zoom processing meeting content (such as AI transcription) will not work.
✘ Phone and SIP Dial-In are Disabled – Participants cannot join via traditional phone lines, as encryption keys are not stored on external devices.
✘ Breakout Rooms are Limited – While possible, they require additional configuration.
✘ Web Client Cannot Join E2EE Meetings – Participants must use the Zoom desktop or mobile app to join.

If these limitations impact your workflow, you may need to decide whether **E2EE is necessary** or if Zoom's standard AES-256 GCM encryption is sufficient.

How to Enable End-to-End Encryption in Zoom

To activate **End-to-End Encryption (E2EE)** for your Zoom meetings, follow these steps:

Step 1: Ensure You Have the Right Account Type

- E2EE is available for Free and Paid Zoom accounts.

- You must have Zoom version 5.4.0 or later to enable E2EE meetings.

Step 2: Enable E2EE in Zoom Settings

1. **Sign in** to your Zoom account via Zoom's web portal.

2. Click on **Settings** in the left-hand navigation menu.

3. Under the **Meetings** tab, scroll down to **Security** settings.

4. Locate the option **End-to-End Encryption** and switch it **ON**.

5. Select **Enabled** and choose the **Default Encryption Type** for new meetings (either **E2EE** or **Enhanced Encryption**).

6. Click **Save Changes**.

💡 **Tip:** If you do not see the option for E2EE, check if your account admin has restricted it.

Step 3: Enable E2EE for a Specific Meeting

Once E2EE is activated in settings, you can **turn it on for specific meetings**:

1. Open the **Zoom app** and go to the **Schedule Meeting** section.

2. In the **Security Settings**, find the **Encryption** option.

3. Select **End-to-End Encryption**.

4. Click **Save** and start your meeting as usual.

How to Verify That E2EE is Active in a Zoom Meeting

When a meeting is secured with E2EE, you will see:
✓☐ A green shield icon with a lock in the top-left corner of the Zoom window.
✓☐ A popup message stating "This meeting is end-to-end encrypted."
✓☐ The ability to verify encryption keys by clicking the shield icon.

💡 **Tip:** If the shield icon is grey instead of green, E2EE is **not active** for that session.

Best Practices for Secure Zoom Meetings

To maximize security, even with E2EE enabled, follow these best practices:

✓ Use Strong Passwords for Meetings – Always set a unique, strong password to prevent unauthorized access.

✓ Enable Waiting Rooms – This allows you to screen participants before admitting them.

✓ Limit Screen Sharing – Only allow hosts or designated participants to share their screens.

✓ Lock the Meeting – Once all participants have joined, lock the session to prevent unwanted intrusions.

✓ Use Zoom's Security Controls – Familiarize yourself with mute, remove participant, and restrict chat options.

By combining E2EE with other security settings, you can create a safe, private, and professional Zoom meeting environment.

Conclusion

Enabling End-to-End Encryption (E2EE) in Zoom meetings provides the highest level of privacy and security for sensitive discussions. While it comes with some functional trade-offs, it ensures that only authorized participants can access meeting content.

By following this guide, you can activate and manage E2EE effectively, ensuring that your meetings remain confidential and protected from external threats.

If you require additional features like cloud recording or phone dial-in, consider using Zoom's standard AES-256 GCM encryption instead.

🔒 **Security Tip:** Regularly update Zoom to the latest version to ensure that you always have the most up-to-date security enhancements.

4.3.2 Managing Meeting Permissions

Introduction

Managing meeting permissions in Zoom is essential for maintaining control over your virtual sessions, ensuring a smooth experience, and protecting against disruptions. Whether you're hosting a business meeting, an online class, or a social gathering, configuring the right permissions can help create a secure and efficient environment. In this section, we will explore the different types of Zoom meeting permissions, how to manage them effectively, and best practices for different scenarios.

Understanding Zoom Meeting Permissions

Zoom provides a range of permissions that allow hosts and co-hosts to control what participants can and cannot do in a meeting. These permissions fall into several categories:

- **Host and Co-host Controls**: The host has full control over the meeting, while co-hosts can manage many features but cannot start or end the meeting.

- **Participant Permissions**: These settings determine what attendees can do, such as screen sharing, using chat, or renaming themselves.

- **Security Features**: Permissions related to authentication, waiting rooms, and removing disruptive participants.

Let's explore each of these in detail.

1. Host and Co-host Permissions

Host Controls

As the host, you have the highest level of control in a Zoom meeting. You can:

- Start and End the Meeting – Only the host can end the meeting for all participants.

- Assign Co-hosts – You can delegate responsibilities to co-hosts, allowing them to help manage the meeting.

- Mute and Unmute Participants – Control the audio settings of individual participants or mute everyone at once.

- Enable or Disable Video – Turn off a participant's camera if needed.

- Lock the Meeting – Prevent new participants from joining once the meeting has started.

- Enable Waiting Room – Control who gets admitted into the meeting.

- Manage Screen Sharing – Decide who can share their screen.

Co-host Controls

A co-host has many of the same permissions as the host, except for the following:

- Cannot start or end the meeting.

- Cannot assign or remove other co-hosts.

- Cannot manage breakout rooms before the meeting starts.

- Cannot start or stop cloud recordings.

Co-hosts are useful for larger meetings, webinars, and virtual classrooms where multiple people need administrative access.

---

2. Participant Permissions

Zoom allows hosts to customize participant permissions to ensure the meeting runs smoothly.

Managing Audio and Video Permissions

- Mute Participants on Entry: Prevents background noise when new attendees join.

- Allow Participants to Unmute Themselves: Useful for interactive sessions, but can be disabled to maintain order.

- Turn Off Video for Participants: Prevents distractions and ensures focus on the main speaker.

Controlling Screen Sharing

By default, Zoom allows the host to share their screen. However, you can modify this:

- Host Only: The safest option for preventing unauthorized sharing.

- All Participants: Useful for collaborative discussions but requires monitoring.

- Enable Annotation Controls: Decide if participants can annotate on shared screens.

Chat and File Sharing Permissions

Zoom's chat feature is valuable for discussions, but improper use can lead to distractions. The host can:

- Disable Chat Entirely

- Restrict Chat to Host Only

- Allow Private Messages (or disable them)

- Enable or Disable File Sharing

3. Security Features and Access Control

Using the Waiting Room Feature

The waiting room allows the host to manually approve participants before they join.

- Admit Participants Individually

- Admit All at Once

- Customize Waiting Room Messages to give attendees instructions.

Locking the Meeting

Once all expected participants have joined, locking the meeting prevents additional people from entering, reducing security risks.

Managing Unauthorized Participants

- Remove Disruptive Attendees – Hosts can eject unwanted guests and prevent them from rejoining.

- Suspend Participant Activities – Temporarily disable all video, audio, and sharing capabilities for everyone in case of disruptions.

4. Best Practices for Managing Meeting Permissions

- Set Default Permissions Before the Meeting: Configure participant settings in advance to prevent disruptions.

- Use Co-hosts for Large Meetings: Assign trusted individuals to help manage participant permissions.

- Regularly Monitor Participant Activity: Keep an eye on the chat, video feeds, and shared screens.

- Encourage Participants to Use Reactions Instead of Unmuting: Helps maintain order in large meetings.

Conclusion

Managing meeting permissions effectively in Zoom ensures a smooth and secure experience for all participants. By leveraging host controls, adjusting participant settings, and utilizing Zoom's security features, you can maintain order and prevent disruptions. Whether you're running a corporate meeting, an educational session, or a social event, properly configured permissions will help create a productive and professional environment.

4.3.3 Handling Zoombombing and Unwanted Guests

Introduction to Zoombombing

Zoombombing refers to the unwanted intrusion of disruptive participants into a Zoom meeting. This phenomenon became widely known during the early days of the COVID-19 pandemic when public Zoom meetings were frequently hijacked by pranksters or malicious users. These individuals often shared inappropriate content, disrupted conversations, or even launched verbal attacks.

Preventing Zoombombing and managing unwanted guests is crucial for maintaining a safe and professional meeting environment. Whether you are hosting a business conference, an educational lecture, or a casual social gathering, implementing proper security measures ensures a smooth and productive session.

This section will provide a detailed guide on how to prevent Zoombombing, remove disruptive participants, and manage security settings effectively.

Understanding How Zoombombing Happens

Before diving into prevention strategies, it is essential to understand how Zoombombing typically occurs. Here are the most common ways intruders gain access to a meeting:

1. Publicly Shared Meeting Links – If a meeting link is shared on social media or public forums, unauthorized users can easily join.

2. Weak Security Settings – Meetings without passcodes or waiting rooms allow anyone with the link to enter freely.

3. Exploited Meeting IDs – If users repeatedly use the same Meeting ID, attackers can guess or find it.

4. Unrestricted Screen Sharing – If screen sharing is enabled for all participants by default, intruders can take control and display unwanted content.

5. Disabling Host Controls – If a host does not monitor participant actions, unwanted guests can cause disruptions.

By understanding these vulnerabilities, hosts can proactively configure their Zoom settings to minimize risks.

Preventing Zoombombing: Best Practices

1. Secure Your Meeting Link and ID

- Avoid Public Sharing: Never post Zoom links on social media or public websites. Instead, share them privately via email or direct messaging.

- Use Random Meeting IDs: Instead of using your Personal Meeting ID (PMI), generate a unique Meeting ID for each session.

- Enable Meeting Passcodes: Set a strong passcode to ensure only invited participants can enter.

2. Enable the Waiting Room Feature

- Approve Participants Before Entry: The Waiting Room allows hosts to screen attendees before letting them into the meeting.

- Customize Waiting Room Messages: Add a note requesting users to provide their full name or email for verification.

- Assign a Co-Host to Manage Entries: If you're leading a large meeting, delegate a co-host to monitor the Waiting Room.

3. Restrict Screen Sharing and Participant Controls

- Limit Screen Sharing to Hosts Only: Prevent unauthorized screen sharing by adjusting the settings under Security > Screen Sharing.

- Disable Annotation for Participants: This prevents intruders from drawing or writing inappropriate content on shared screens.

- Turn Off File Sharing in Chat: Prevent unwanted files from being shared to avoid inappropriate content or malware.

4. Lock the Meeting After Everyone Joins

- Use the "Lock Meeting" Feature: Once all expected participants have joined, go to Security > Lock Meeting to prevent new users from entering.

- Set a Registration Requirement: Require participants to register with their email before receiving the meeting link.

5. Enable Advanced Security Settings

- Restrict Participants from Renaming Themselves: This prevents intruders from changing their display names to impersonate someone else.

- Disable "Join Before Host": This ensures that no one can start the meeting before you arrive.

- Enable Two-Factor Authentication (2FA) for Zoom Accounts: This adds an extra layer of security to prevent unauthorized account access.

Managing Unwanted Guests During a Meeting

Even with strong security measures, unwanted guests may still find ways to enter. If this happens, take the following steps immediately:

1. Remove the Intruder

- Click on **Participants** > **Find the Intruder** > **Remove**.

- Alternatively, click on **Security** > **Remove Participant**.

- Once removed, the user **cannot** rejoin unless you adjust settings.

2. Mute and Disable Video

- Click on **Participants** > **Mute All** to stop disruptions.
- Turn off the intruder's video to prevent inappropriate visuals.

3. Disable Chat and Screen Sharing Temporarily

- If the intruder is posting spam in chat, click **Chat > Host Only** to limit messages.
- If the intruder is sharing inappropriate content, disable screen sharing immediately.

4. Lock the Meeting

- Click **Security > Lock Meeting** to prevent further intrusions.

5. Report the User to Zoom

- Click on **Participants > More > Report** to send a complaint to Zoom.
- Include details about the intrusion, such as offensive content or behavior.

Post-Meeting Security Actions

1. Review Meeting Settings

- After a Zoombombing incident, review your security settings to prevent future occurrences.
- Check the meeting log to identify how the intruder gained access.

2. Report Serious Incidents to Zoom and Authorities

- If the intrusion involved threats, harassment, or illegal activity, report the incident to Zoom Support.
- In severe cases, consider reporting to local authorities.

3. Educate Participants on Security Best Practices

- Send follow-up emails or messages reminding attendees about **safe meeting practices**.

- Share resources on how to secure Zoom meetings effectively.

Conclusion: Maintaining a Secure Zoom Environment

Preventing Zoombombing and managing unwanted guests requires a combination of strong security settings, proactive monitoring, and quick response actions. By implementing the strategies outlined in this section, you can ensure that your Zoom meetings remain safe, professional, and disruption-free.

Key Takeaways

✓ Always use passcodes, waiting rooms, and meeting locks to secure access.

✓ Limit participant controls by restricting screen sharing, chat, and renaming.

✓ Act quickly to remove intruders, mute disruptions, and report incidents.

✓ Regularly update your Zoom security settings to protect against new threats.

By following these best practices, you can confidently host Zoom meetings without the risk of unwanted interruptions. Stay secure, stay professional, and enjoy smooth virtual meetings!

CHAPTER V
Best Practices for Effective Zoom Meetings

5.1 Preparing for a Professional Meeting

5.1.1 Optimizing Lighting and Background

Creating a professional and visually appealing setup is crucial for an effective Zoom meeting. Poor lighting and distracting backgrounds can make you appear unprofessional and disengaged, negatively impacting your communication. In this section, we will explore best practices for optimizing lighting and background to ensure you present yourself in the best possible way.

1. Importance of Good Lighting in Zoom Meetings

Lighting plays a crucial role in how you appear on camera. Poor lighting can create shadows, make you look washed out, or cause distractions. Here's why good lighting matters:

- **Enhances Visibility** – Well-lit faces are easier to see, ensuring clear communication.

- **Improves Professionalism** – Proper lighting conveys a polished and professional look.

- **Prevents Eye Strain** – Balanced lighting reduces glare and strain on viewers' eyes.

- **Boosts Engagement** – When people can see your facial expressions clearly, they feel more connected.

2. Best Practices for Optimizing Lighting

2.1 Natural vs. Artificial Lighting

Understanding different types of lighting sources will help you choose the best setup for your Zoom meetings.

Natural Light

- **Advantages**: Provides soft, even lighting that enhances your appearance.

- **Disadvantages**: Dependent on time of day and weather conditions.

- **Best Practices**:

    o Position yourself **facing a window** to take advantage of natural light.

    o Avoid **sitting with a window behind you**, as this will cause backlighting, making your face appear dark.

    o Use **curtains or blinds** to diffuse harsh sunlight and prevent overexposure.

Artificial Light

- **Advantages**: Consistent and controllable lighting.

- **Disadvantages**: Can create harsh shadows or unflattering tones if not set up correctly.

- **Best Practices**:

    o Use **soft, warm LED lights** for a balanced, professional look.

    o Position **lights at a 45-degree angle** on both sides of your face to reduce shadows.

    o Avoid overhead lighting, which can create unflattering shadows under your eyes.

    o Consider using a **ring light** or **softbox light** for even illumination.

2.2 Lighting Placement Techniques

Proper placement of lights ensures that your face is well-lit without harsh shadows.

Three-Point Lighting Setup

A professional lighting technique commonly used in video production and Zoom meetings.

1. **Key Light** – The main light source, placed slightly to one side of your face.

2. **Fill Light** – A softer light placed on the opposite side to reduce shadows.

3. **Back Light** – Positioned behind you to add depth and prevent you from blending into the background.

Alternative Budget-Friendly Lighting Setups

If professional lighting is not available, you can use everyday household lamps:

- Use a **desk lamp with a soft LED bulb** positioned at eye level.

- Reflect light off a **white wall or ceiling** for a softer effect.

- Adjust **brightness and color temperature** to match natural skin tones.

---

3. Choosing the Right Background for Zoom Meetings

Your background plays a significant role in maintaining a professional appearance. A cluttered or distracting background can reduce engagement and shift focus away from your message.

3.1 Types of Zoom Meeting Backgrounds

1. Real Backgrounds

A real background can provide authenticity but requires careful arrangement. **Best Practices:**

- Keep the background **clean and uncluttered**.

- Use a **plain wall** or a well-organized bookshelf for a professional appearance.

- Ensure there are no distracting objects, such as laundry or personal items.

- Maintain a **consistent theme** that aligns with your profession (e.g., a study for educators, a clean office for business meetings).

2. Virtual Backgrounds

Zoom allows users to replace their real background with a digital one. **Best Practices:**

- Choose a **subtle, professional background** (e.g., a simple office space).

- Avoid overly bright or animated backgrounds, as they can be distracting.

- Use a **green screen** for better background blending.

- Ensure adequate lighting to prevent glitches around your face and hair.

3. Blurred Background

A blurred background helps maintain privacy while keeping the focus on you. **Best Practices:**

- Use Zoom's **built-in blur feature** for a polished effect.

- Avoid moving too much, as excessive movement can cause blurring distortions.

4. Common Lighting and Background Mistakes to Avoid

Even with the right setup, small mistakes can ruin the quality of your video. Here are some common pitfalls and how to avoid them.

4.1 Lighting Mistakes

✘ **Backlighting** – Sitting with a window behind you makes your face appear dark. ✓ **Solution**: Face the light source instead of having it behind you.

✘ **Uneven Lighting** – Shadows on one side of the face can make you look unbalanced. ✓ **Solution**: Use multiple light sources or soft light reflectors.

✘ **Harsh Overhead Lights** – Creates unflattering shadows under the eyes and chin. ✓ **Solution**: Use side lighting or a soft diffused light source.

4.2 Background Mistakes

✘ **Cluttered Backgrounds** – Too many items behind you distract viewers. ✓ **Solution**: Declutter and organize the space behind you.

✘ **Overly Bright Virtual Backgrounds** – Bright or animated backgrounds can be distracting.
✔ **Solution**: Choose a simple, professional virtual background.

✘ **Mismatched Themes** – A casual or messy background can look unprofessional.
✔ **Solution**: Keep your background in line with the meeting's tone.

5. Recommended Equipment for Lighting and Background Optimization

If you frequently host Zoom meetings, investing in proper equipment can significantly enhance your video quality.

5.1 Recommended Lighting Equipment

💡 **Ring Light** – Ideal for evenly lighting your face without harsh shadows.
💡 **Softbox Light** – Provides diffused light for a professional look.
💡 **Desk Lamp with Adjustable Brightness** – A budget-friendly alternative.

5.2 Recommended Background Equipment

☐☐ **Green Screen** – Improves the quality of virtual backgrounds.
☐☐ **Portable Backdrop** – Helps create a clean and consistent background.
☐☐ **Bookshelf or Office Setup** – A natural, professional setting for meetings.

6. Final Tips for Perfecting Your Zoom Setup

To ensure a flawless presentation in every Zoom meeting, follow these final recommendations:

✔ Test Your Setup Before Meetings – Adjust lighting and background in advance.
✔ Use Zoom's Preview Feature – Check your appearance before joining the meeting.
✔ Balance Lighting and Background – Make sure neither is too bright nor too dark.
✔ Maintain a Professional Presence – Position yourself centrally and maintain eye contact with the camera.

By optimizing your **lighting and background**, you can significantly enhance your presence in Zoom meetings, making your communication more professional, engaging, and effective.

5.1.2 Choosing the Right Audio Setup

Introduction

Audio quality is one of the most crucial aspects of a successful Zoom meeting. Poor audio can lead to misunderstandings, frustration, and disengagement among participants. Whether you're hosting a professional business meeting, an online class, or a social gathering, choosing the right audio setup ensures clear communication and an optimal experience for all attendees.

This section explores the different types of audio setups, best practices for improving sound quality, troubleshooting common issues, and recommendations for various use cases. By the end, you will have a comprehensive understanding of how to optimize your audio for professional Zoom meetings.

1. Understanding Audio Devices for Zoom

Before choosing the right audio setup, it's essential to understand the various devices available for capturing and transmitting sound in a Zoom meeting.

1.1 Built-in Microphones and Speakers

Most laptops, smartphones, and tablets come with built-in microphones and speakers. While convenient, these built-in devices often lack high-quality noise cancellation and sensitivity, leading to background noise, echo, and muffled audio.

✅ **Pros:**

- No additional equipment needed
- Easy to use and set up
- Works well for casual meetings

✖ **Cons:**

- Lower audio quality
- Prone to picking up background noise
- Echo and feedback issues in larger meetings

1.2 External USB or Wireless Microphones

External microphones provide better sound quality by focusing on the speaker's voice while reducing background noise. USB microphones are plug-and-play devices that connect easily to your computer, while wireless microphones allow more flexibility in movement.

✅ **Pros:**

- Superior sound quality compared to built-in microphones
- Better background noise reduction
- Ideal for professional meetings and presentations

✖ **Cons:**

- Requires additional setup and investment
- May need drivers or software configuration

1.3 Headsets with Microphones

A wired or wireless headset with a built-in microphone is a popular choice for professionals who attend frequent Zoom meetings. These headsets offer improved sound quality and noise isolation, ensuring that both you and your audience hear each other clearly.

✅ **Pros:**

- Excellent noise isolation
- Eliminates echo and feedback
- Comfortable for long meetings

✖ **Cons:**

- Some models can be bulky or uncomfortable over extended use
- Wireless headsets may require charging

1.4 Conference Speakerphones

For group meetings in a physical conference room, a dedicated conference speakerphone (such as a Zoom-certified speakerphone) provides omnidirectional microphone coverage and high-quality sound.

✅ **Pros:**

- Optimized for group conversations

- High-quality microphone and speaker combination

- Reduces background noise effectively

❌ **Cons:**

- Expensive compared to other options

- Requires a stable power source and configuration

2. Choosing the Best Audio Setup Based on Your Use Case

Different meeting environments require different audio setups. Here are the best recommendations based on specific Zoom meeting scenarios:

2.1 Solo Meetings or One-on-One Calls

For personal meetings or one-on-one calls, a high-quality headset with a microphone is the best option. If using a built-in microphone, ensure that you are in a quiet environment.

Recommended Setup:

- Wired or wireless headset with a noise-canceling microphone

- USB external microphone for better voice clarity

- Quiet room with minimal background noise

2.2 Business Meetings and Webinars

For professional settings, external microphones or high-quality headsets are crucial. If you are presenting to a large audience, a dedicated podcast-style microphone or a conference speakerphone may be ideal.

Recommended Setup:

- USB condenser microphone for better voice clarity

- Wireless headset for flexibility

- Noise-canceling headphones to block distractions

2.3 Online Classes and Training Sessions

Teachers and trainers need to ensure clear, consistent audio to maintain engagement and effective communication. A wireless microphone or headset can offer mobility while teaching.

Recommended Setup:

- Wireless lapel microphone for hands-free speaking

- Headset with a boom mic for better voice capture

- Echo cancellation software if teaching in a large space

2.4 Large Team or Conference Room Meetings

For hybrid meetings where multiple participants are in the same room, a conference speakerphone with omnidirectional microphones is the best choice.

Recommended Setup:

- Zoom-certified conference speakerphone

- Multiple microphones for large conference rooms

- Acoustic paneling or soundproofing for better audio quality

3. Optimizing Audio Settings in Zoom

Once you have chosen the right hardware, configuring Zoom settings is the next step to achieving the best audio quality.

3.1 Adjusting Audio Input and Output

To select the correct microphone and speaker:

1. Open **Zoom Settings** (Click the gear icon in the Zoom app).

2. Navigate to **Audio** settings.

3. Under **Microphone**, select your preferred microphone from the dropdown menu.

4. Under **Speaker**, choose the best output device (e.g., external speakers, headset).

5. Click **Test Mic** and **Test Speaker** to ensure proper audio levels.

3.2 Enabling Noise Suppression

Zoom offers built-in noise suppression to eliminate background noise:

- Navigate to **Audio Settings > Suppress Background Noise**

- Choose **High** for professional meetings to block keyboard clicks, fan noise, and other distractions.

3.3 Using Push-to-Talk Feature

For larger meetings, enabling **Push-to-Talk** allows you to stay muted by default and unmute yourself only when speaking:

1. Go to **Audio Settings**

2. Enable **Press and hold SPACE key to temporarily unmute yourself**

3.4 Using Zoom's Echo Cancellation

To prevent echo and feedback:

- Use headphones instead of built-in speakers

- Keep your microphone away from your speakers

- Enable **Zoom Echo Cancellation** in the **Audio Settings**

---

4. Troubleshooting Common Audio Problems

Even with a proper setup, audio issues can still arise. Here are common problems and how to fix them:

4.1 Microphone Not Working

Solution:

- Ensure the correct microphone is selected in Zoom.

- Check if the microphone is muted or disabled in your system settings.

- Restart Zoom or your computer.

4.2 Background Noise and Echo

Solution:

- Use a noise-canceling microphone or headset.

- Enable **High Noise Suppression** in Zoom settings.

- Reduce the volume of external speakers.

4.3 Audio Delay or Distortion

Solution:

- Close unnecessary applications using system resources.

- Use a wired internet connection instead of Wi-Fi.

- Lower Zoom's **Original Sound** feature if experiencing distortion.

Conclusion

Selecting the right audio setup for Zoom meetings is essential for maintaining professionalism and ensuring clear communication. Whether you are attending a solo meeting, hosting a webinar, teaching an online class, or conducting a team meeting, investing in the right audio equipment and optimizing Zoom settings can significantly improve your virtual meeting experience.

By implementing the best practices outlined in this section, you can eliminate background noise, avoid audio disruptions, and create an engaging and productive meeting environment. Remember, clear audio leads to clear communication, and clear communication leads to successful meetings.

5.1.3 Setting Up an Agenda

Introduction

A well-structured agenda is the backbone of an effective Zoom meeting. Without a clear agenda, meetings can become disorganized, unfocused, and inefficient, leading to wasted time and reduced engagement. Whether you're hosting a business meeting, an educational session, or a personal gathering, setting up an agenda ensures that everyone knows what to expect, stays on track, and contributes meaningfully to the discussion.

In this section, we will explore the importance of having an agenda, how to create one, and best practices for keeping your meeting productive and goal-oriented.

Why an Agenda is Essential for Zoom Meetings

An agenda serves several critical purposes:

1. **Provides Structure and Clarity** – It outlines the key topics to be discussed and the order in which they will be covered.

2. **Improves Time Management** – Helps keep the meeting within the allocated time by setting clear boundaries for each topic.

3. **Enhances Engagement and Participation** – Participants know what to expect and can prepare in advance, leading to more meaningful contributions.

4. **Reduces Unnecessary Discussions** – Keeps the meeting focused and prevents side conversations or unrelated discussions from taking over.

5. **Ensures Accountability** – Assigning responsibilities within the agenda helps team members stay accountable for their tasks and follow-ups.

Without an agenda, meetings can easily become chaotic, with discussions meandering off course, making it difficult to achieve intended goals.

Steps to Create an Effective Agenda

Step 1: Define the Meeting Objectives

Before drafting an agenda, ask yourself:

- What is the primary purpose of this meeting?

- What outcomes do I want to achieve by the end of it?

- Who needs to be involved, and what are their roles?

For example, a **team meeting** might focus on project updates, while a **client meeting** could be about discussing deliverables and gathering feedback. Having a clear objective ensures that the agenda remains relevant and results-driven.

Step 2: Identify Key Discussion Points

List the main topics that need to be covered during the meeting. Consider the following:

- **Priority Items** – Topics that require immediate attention or decision-making.

- **Regular Updates** – Recurring discussions such as project status reports or performance reviews.

- **New Business** – Any new initiatives, challenges, or opportunities to discuss.

For a **business team meeting**, a sample agenda might include:

1. Welcome and brief introduction (5 mins)

2. Team updates (10 mins)

3. Review of project milestones (15 mins)

4. Discussion on upcoming challenges (15 mins)

5. Action items and next steps (10 mins)

Step 3: Assign Time Limits to Each Topic

One of the biggest challenges in meetings is staying on schedule. Assigning time limits ensures that no single topic dominates the discussion.

For example:

- **Status updates** – 5 minutes per team member

- **Decision-making discussions** – 15 minutes

- **Q&A session** – 10 minutes

Using a timer or Zoom's built-in **timekeeper tools** can help maintain discipline and avoid overruns.

Step 4: Assign Roles and Responsibilities

Clearly define who will lead each section of the agenda. Typical roles include:

- **Host/Moderator** – The person responsible for running the meeting and keeping discussions on track.

- **Presenters** – Individuals assigned to lead specific topics.

- **Note-taker** – Responsible for recording key decisions and action items.

- **Timekeeper** – Ensures that discussions adhere to the allocated time.

Having assigned roles prevents meetings from being dominated by a single person and ensures everyone is actively engaged.

Step 5: Share the Agenda in Advance

Distribute the agenda **at least 24 hours** before the meeting to give participants time to prepare.

Methods of sharing the agenda:

- **Email** – Send the agenda in a well-structured email.

- **Google Docs or Microsoft OneNote** – Allows real-time collaboration.

- **Zoom Meeting Invitation** – Include key discussion points in the calendar invite.

Encourage attendees to review the agenda beforehand and come prepared with any necessary data or questions.

Best Practices for an Effective Zoom Meeting Agenda

1. Keep It Concise and Focused

Avoid overloading the agenda with too many topics. A well-structured agenda should focus on essential points that contribute to the meeting's objective.

2. Allow Time for Participant Contributions

Encourage interaction by allocating time for open discussion or Q&A sessions. This fosters engagement and ensures everyone's input is valued.

3. Use Visual Aids and Shared Documents

If your meeting involves presentations or reports, attach relevant files to the agenda so attendees can review them in advance. Use **Zoom's screen-sharing feature** to display important documents during discussions.

4. Build in Flexibility for Unforeseen Topics

Sometimes unexpected issues arise. Having a few minutes reserved at the end for additional discussion ensures that urgent matters can be addressed without disrupting the meeting flow.

5. Follow Up with Action Items

At the end of the meeting, summarize key takeaways and assign action items with deadlines. Use a **shared document or project management tool** to track progress and accountability.

Sample Zoom Meeting Agenda Templates

Example 1: Business Team Meeting

Meeting Title: Weekly Team Check-in
Objective: Review project progress and upcoming deadlines
Time: 10:00 AM – 11:00 AM (60 mins)

Time	Topic	Speaker
10:00 AM – 10:05 AM	Welcome and Introductions	Host
10:05 AM – 10:20 AM	Team Updates	All team members
10:20 AM – 10:35 AM	Review of Ongoing Projects	Project Manager
10:35 AM – 10:50 AM	Discussion on Challenges & Solutions	Open Discussion
10:50 AM – 11:00 AM	Action Items and Next Steps	Host

Example 2: Educational Webinar

Meeting Title: Effective Time Management for Students
Objective: Teach students time management techniques
Time: 3:00 PM – 4:30 PM (90 mins)

Time	Topic	Speaker
3:00 PM – 3:10 PM	Welcome and Agenda Overview	Host
3:10 PM – 3:40 PM	Understanding Time Management	Presenter
3:40 PM – 4:00 PM	Interactive Q&A Session	Open Discussion
4:00 PM – 4:30 PM	Hands-on Activity: Planning Your Week	Host

Conclusion

A well-prepared agenda is essential for ensuring that Zoom meetings are **efficient, engaging, and goal-oriented**. By clearly defining objectives, structuring discussion topics, assigning time limits, and sharing the agenda in advance, hosts can create meetings that maximize productivity while keeping participants actively involved.

The next time you plan a Zoom meeting, use these strategies to **set up a professional agenda** and keep your discussions on track. A well-structured agenda doesn't just save time—it makes your meetings more impactful and meaningful.

5.2 Engaging Participants

5.2.1 Encouraging Interaction and Participation

In a virtual setting like Zoom, keeping participants engaged can be challenging. Unlike in-person meetings, where physical presence naturally fosters attention and engagement, online meetings require intentional efforts to encourage interaction. This section explores various strategies, tools, and best practices to ensure that attendees stay actively involved throughout your Zoom meetings.

1. The Importance of Engagement in Virtual Meetings

Engagement is the key to a successful Zoom meeting. When participants are actively involved, they are more likely to absorb information, contribute valuable insights, and collaborate effectively. A lack of engagement can lead to distractions, reduced productivity, and disengagement from key discussions.

Challenges of Virtual Engagement

- **Distractions:** Participants may be multitasking, checking emails, or dealing with background noise.

- **Lack of Non-Verbal Cues:** It is harder to read facial expressions, making it difficult to gauge engagement levels.

- **Passivity:** Some attendees may feel uncomfortable speaking up in virtual settings.

- **Zoom Fatigue:** Long hours on Zoom can cause exhaustion, making it harder to stay engaged.

By addressing these challenges, you can create a more interactive and productive Zoom meeting experience.

2. Preparing an Interactive Zoom Meeting

Engagement starts with preparation. Before the meeting begins, take proactive steps to create an environment that encourages participation.

Setting Clear Objectives

A well-structured meeting with clear objectives helps attendees stay focused. Define what you want to achieve and communicate these goals to participants in advance. For example:

- "By the end of this meeting, we should finalize the project timeline."

- "Today, we will brainstorm ideas for the upcoming marketing campaign."

Choosing the Right Format

Not all meetings should follow the traditional speaker-listener format. Consider interactive formats such as:

- **Roundtable discussions:** Each participant takes turns sharing insights.

- **Breakout room discussions:** Smaller groups engage in focused conversations.

- **Panel discussions:** A few selected participants lead discussions while others contribute through chat or Q&A.

Creating an Agenda with Interactive Elements

Structure your agenda to include moments for interaction. Example:

- **5 minutes:** Icebreaker question

- **15 minutes:** Presentation with interactive polling

- **20 minutes:** Group discussion in breakout rooms

- **10 minutes:** Q&A session

By weaving interactive elements into the agenda, you set expectations for participation.

3. Encouraging Active Participation During the Meeting

Once the meeting starts, focus on fostering engagement through different techniques and Zoom features.

Using Icebreakers to Set the Tone

Icebreakers help create a relaxed atmosphere, especially when attendees don't know each other well. Examples:

- **Fun question:** "If you could work from anywhere in the world, where would it be?"

- **Two truths and a lie:** Each person states two facts and one lie about themselves, and others guess the lie.

- **Virtual background challenge:** Ask participants to use a background that represents their mood or interests.

Encouraging Verbal Participation

Some attendees hesitate to speak in virtual meetings. Encourage verbal interaction by:

- **Asking direct questions:** Instead of saying, "Any thoughts?" try, "John, what do you think about this proposal?"

- **Rotating speakers:** Assign different participants to present sections of the meeting.

- **Encouraging opinions:** Use phrases like, "I'd love to hear different perspectives on this."

Leveraging Zoom Chat for Engagement

For those who prefer not to speak, chat offers a great alternative:

- **Ask questions and encourage responses in chat.** Example: "Type 'yes' if you agree, or share your opinion in the chat."

- **Use chat for brainstorming.** Ask participants to list ideas quickly, then discuss them as a group.

- **Acknowledge and respond to chat messages.** This ensures participants feel heard.

Using Polls to Gather Instant Feedback

Zoom's polling feature allows you to quickly gauge opinions. Example poll questions:

- "How confident do you feel about the new strategy? (Very Confident – Not Confident)"

- "What topic should we prioritize for the next meeting?"

Poll results provide real-time insights and make participants feel their input matters.

Utilizing Reactions and Emojis

Encourage participants to use Zoom's reactions to show engagement:

- 👍 (Thumbs up) – Agreement

- 👏 (Clapping) – Appreciation

- 🫤 (Thinking face) – Uncertainty or curiosity

This adds an interactive element without disrupting the conversation.

4. Enhancing Engagement with Zoom Breakout Rooms

Breakout rooms are excellent for group discussions and teamwork.

When to Use Breakout Rooms

- Brainstorming sessions: Small groups generate ideas and report back.

- Training sessions: Participants practice skills in a smaller setting.

- Team collaboration: Groups work on tasks independently before rejoining the main meeting.

Best Practices for Breakout Rooms

- Give clear instructions before splitting groups. Example: "In your breakout rooms, discuss the top three challenges your team is facing."

- Assign a facilitator for each room to keep discussions on track.

- Set a time limit so discussions remain focused.

After returning from breakout rooms, ask one person per group to summarize their discussion.

5. Managing Q&A Sessions Effectively

The Q&A segment is a key moment for interaction.

Encouraging Questions

- Ask open-ended questions like, "What are your thoughts on this approach?"

- Create a 'parking lot' for unanswered questions to address them later.

Structuring the Q&A Segment

- Live questions: Let participants unmute themselves and ask questions.

- Chat-based Q&A: Attendees type questions, and the host reads them aloud.

- Pre-submitted questions: Collect questions before the meeting and answer them systematically.

Handling Difficult Questions

- If you don't know the answer: Acknowledge it and promise to follow up.

- If a question is off-topic: Redirect it to another time. Example: "That's a great point! Let's address it separately after the meeting."

---

6. Overcoming Engagement Challenges

Even with the best efforts, some participants may remain disengaged.

Identifying Signs of Disengagement

- Lack of responses to questions

- Minimal participation in discussions

- Cameras turned off for extended periods

Strategies to Re-Engage Participants

- Call on individuals by name (without putting them on the spot).

- Use humor and storytelling to keep the discussion lively.

- Adjust the pace if the meeting feels too slow or fast.

Avoiding Common Mistakes

- Talking too much without pauses. Instead, create moments for input.

- Skipping engagement features like polls and breakout rooms.

- Ignoring chat messages or reactions. Respond actively to build interaction.

7. Conclusion: Creating Engaging Zoom Meetings

Encouraging interaction and participation in Zoom meetings requires planning, creativity, and flexibility. To recap:

- Prepare in advance with a structured, interactive agenda.

- Leverage Zoom's engagement tools such as chat, reactions, polls, and breakout rooms.

- Encourage verbal participation through direct questions and interactive discussions.

- Create a welcoming and inclusive atmosphere where every participant feels valued.

By applying these techniques, you can transform your Zoom meetings from passive, one-sided presentations into dynamic, interactive experiences that keep participants engaged and productive.

5.2.2 Using Visual Aids Effectively

Visual aids play a crucial role in making Zoom meetings engaging, informative, and impactful. Whether you are delivering a business presentation, conducting a virtual training session, or teaching an online class, the right use of visuals can enhance communication, improve understanding, and keep participants focused. In this section, we will explore different types of visual aids, best practices for using them effectively, and common mistakes to avoid.

1. Why Are Visual Aids Important in Zoom Meetings?

Visual aids serve multiple purposes in virtual meetings, including:

- **Enhancing comprehension** – Images, graphs, and charts simplify complex ideas.

- **Keeping participants engaged** – Well-designed visuals capture attention and reduce screen fatigue.

- **Reinforcing key messages** – Visuals provide clarity and help reinforce the most critical points.

- **Encouraging participation** – Interactive visual aids, such as whiteboards or live polling, promote engagement.

- **Making content memorable** – People tend to remember visuals better than text-heavy content.

Given the challenges of remote communication, using visual aids correctly can significantly improve the effectiveness of your Zoom meetings.

2. Types of Visual Aids for Zoom Meetings

There are various types of visual aids you can use, depending on your objectives and audience.

2.1 Slide Decks (PowerPoint, Google Slides, Keynote)

Slide presentations are the most commonly used visual aid in virtual meetings. They allow you to structure your content and present it in an organized, engaging manner.

Best Practices for Slide Design:

- Keep slides simple – Avoid clutter and excessive text. Aim for a 6x6 rule (six lines per slide, six words per line).

- Use high-quality images – Relevant visuals improve engagement and understanding.

- Maintain consistent formatting – Use a uniform font style and color scheme.

- Add minimal animations – Subtle transitions help guide attention but avoid overuse.

- Include charts and infographics – Data visualization simplifies complex information.

2.2 Screen Sharing Documents and Web Pages

Instead of static slides, you can share live documents or web pages during a meeting. This is useful for:

- Reviewing reports, proposals, or contracts in real time.

- Collaborating on a shared document (Google Docs, Microsoft Word, etc.).

- Demonstrating a live website or online tool.

Best Practices:

- Close unnecessary tabs and notifications – Prevent distractions when sharing your screen.

- Use Zoom's annotation tool – Highlight key sections while presenting documents.

- Check document permissions – Ensure that participants can access shared files.

2.3 Virtual Whiteboards (Zoom Whiteboard, Miro, MURAL, Microsoft Whiteboard)

Whiteboards help brainstorm ideas, illustrate concepts, and enhance collaboration.

Best Practices for Using a Whiteboard:

- Pre-plan your whiteboard structure – Sketch a rough outline of what you want to present.

- Encourage participant interaction – Allow team members to contribute in real time.

- Use different colors and shapes – Highlight important information for clarity.

- Save and share the whiteboard – Zoom allows you to save whiteboard sessions for reference.

2.4 Video Clips and GIFs

Short videos can be an excellent way to explain concepts, demonstrate a product, or break up long meetings.

Best Practices for Using Video in Zoom:

- Keep videos under two minutes – Shorter clips maintain attention and avoid disruptions.

- Ensure good audio quality – Poor sound can distract from your message.

- Use video sparingly – Too many videos can disrupt the meeting flow.

- Test playback before the meeting – Ensure the video plays smoothly within Zoom.

2.5 Live Demonstrations and Product Walkthroughs

For training sessions, live demos of software or products can be more effective than pre-recorded videos.

Best Practices for Live Demos:

- Prepare a step-by-step plan – Know exactly what you want to showcase.
- Use Zoom's spotlight feature – This keeps the focus on your video feed.
- Engage with questions – Allow participants to ask questions throughout the demo.

3. Technical Considerations for Using Visual Aids on Zoom

Even well-designed visual aids can fail if technical issues arise. Here are some key factors to consider:

Internet Connection Stability

- Ensure a stable internet connection to prevent lags when sharing visual content.
- Use **wired connections** instead of Wi-Fi when possible.
- Close unnecessary applications to free up bandwidth.

Screen Resolution and Display Settings

- Optimize screen resolution to prevent blurry visuals.
- Use **full-screen mode** when presenting slides.
- Adjust font size so that text is readable on different devices.

Audio-Visual Synchronization

- If using video clips, test **audio-video sync** before the meeting.
- Check **Zoom's "Optimize for Video" setting** when sharing videos.

4. Common Mistakes to Avoid When Using Visual Aids

Overloading Slides with Text

- Too much text can overwhelm participants.

- Break information into smaller, digestible points.

Using Distracting or Unreadable Fonts

- Avoid overly decorative fonts that are hard to read.

- Stick to professional, high-contrast color schemes.

Neglecting Engagement During Visual Presentations

- Don't just read off slides—add commentary and ask questions.

- Use interactive elements like polls, chat discussions, or reactions.

Technical Failures Due to Poor Preparation

- Always test slides, videos, and whiteboards before a meeting.

- Have a backup plan (e.g., PDF copies of slides in case of technical issues).

5. Interactive Strategies for Maximizing Visual Aid Impact

To make your Zoom meetings truly engaging, combine visual aids with interactive elements such as:

Polls and Surveys

- Conduct quick polls to gauge audience opinions.

- Use tools like Zoom Polls, Mentimeter, or Slido.

Annotations and Live Markups

- Encourage participants to use Zoom's annotation tools to mark slides.

- Use a stylus or drawing tool to highlight key points.

Breakout Room Discussions Based on Visual Content

- After presenting a concept, send participants into breakout rooms to discuss.

- Have them use a shared Google Doc or virtual whiteboard to capture ideas.

Conclusion: Mastering the Art of Visual Presentations on Zoom

Using visual aids effectively is not just about adding slides or videos—it's about delivering information in a way that **engages, educates, and inspires** participants. By following best practices, avoiding common pitfalls, and leveraging interactive tools, you can transform your Zoom meetings into **highly engaging experiences** that drive better understanding and collaboration.

Key Takeaways:

✓ Keep visuals **simple, relevant, and engaging**.
✓ **Test all visual aids** before the meeting.
✓ Use **interactive elements** to make presentations dynamic.
✓ Ensure **technical stability** for smooth delivery.

By mastering these techniques, you'll not only improve the quality of your Zoom presentations but also **leave a lasting impact on your audience**.

5.2.3 Managing Q&A Sessions

In any Zoom meeting, whether it's a business presentation, a webinar, an educational session, or a team discussion, managing the Q&A (Questions and Answers) segment effectively is crucial for engagement and clarity. A well-handled Q&A session enhances interaction, ensures the audience's concerns are addressed, and provides additional value beyond the main presentation.

This section will guide you through the best practices for managing Q&A sessions in Zoom meetings, covering everything from setting up Q&A tools to moderating and responding to questions efficiently.

1. Understanding the Importance of Q&A Sessions

1.1 Why Q&A Sessions Matter

A well-structured Q&A session allows attendees to:

- Gain deeper insights into the topic being discussed.

- Clarify doubts that may not have been covered in the main presentation.

- Feel engaged and valued as active participants in the meeting.

- Foster discussion and idea exchange, making the meeting more interactive.

For hosts and speakers, Q&A sessions provide an opportunity to:

- Address audience concerns directly.

- Reinforce key points from the presentation.

- Gauge audience understanding and interest.

- Build credibility and authority in the subject matter.

1.2 Types of Q&A Formats in Zoom

Depending on the nature of your Zoom meeting, you can choose from different Q&A formats:

- **Live Open Q&A:** Participants can unmute themselves and ask questions verbally.

- **Chat-Based Q&A:** Attendees type their questions in the Zoom chat box.

- **Dedicated Q&A Panel (for Webinars):** A structured Q&A tool where questions are submitted and reviewed before being addressed.

- **Pre-Collected Questions:** Gathering questions before the meeting through emails or surveys and answering them during the session.

Each format has its advantages and is suitable for different meeting types.

2. Setting Up Q&A Sessions in Zoom

2.1 Enabling and Configuring the Q&A Feature

For **Zoom Meetings:**

1. Ensure the chat function is enabled in **Zoom Settings** before the meeting.

2. Decide whether participants can send questions to everyone or just the host.

3. Assign a co-host or moderator to help filter questions if necessary.

For **Zoom Webinars:**

1. Use the **Q&A feature** in the webinar settings.

2. Choose whether attendees can see all submitted questions or only answered ones.

3. Enable the **upvote feature** so participants can prioritize popular questions.

2.2 Using Chat, Polls, and Reactions for Q&A

- Encourage participants to type questions in the **chat box** throughout the session.

- Use **polls** to gauge audience interest in specific discussion points.

- Ask attendees to use **reactions (👍, ✋, etc.)** to indicate agreement with a question.

3. Best Practices for Managing Q&A Sessions

3.1 Structuring the Q&A Segment

To maintain order and engagement, consider structuring your Q&A session:

- **Designate a Specific Q&A Time:** Allocate time at the end or after key sections of your presentation.

- **Set Clear Guidelines:** Inform participants at the beginning about how they can ask questions.

- **Limit Response Time:** Keep answers concise to accommodate more questions.

3.2 Moderating the Q&A Effectively

- **Have a Co-Host or Moderator:** If handling a large audience, assign a moderator to filter and read questions.

- **Group Similar Questions Together:** Avoid redundancy and ensure broader topics are covered.

- **Prioritize Relevant and Popular Questions:** Use the Zoom webinar **upvote feature** or manually select key questions.

3.3 Encouraging Participation

- **Acknowledge Good Questions:** Thank participants for asking.

- **Use Names When Answering:** This personalizes responses and boosts engagement.

- **Encourage Follow-Ups:** If a response requires more detail, direct participants to additional resources or follow-up discussions.

4. Handling Difficult Situations in Q&A Sessions

Managing Off-Topic Questions

- Politely redirect the discussion:

  - "That's a great question, but it's slightly outside today's topic. Let's connect later to discuss this further."

Dealing with Negative or Disruptive Questions

- Stay professional and composed.

- If a question is inappropriate, ignore it or provide a neutral response.

- Mute or remove disruptive participants if necessary.

Handling Time Constraints

- If time is short, select high-priority questions.

- Offer to answer remaining questions via email or a follow-up session.

5. Wrapping Up the Q&A Session

Summarizing Key Takeaways

- Recap important questions and answers.

- Highlight the most frequently asked concerns.

Closing on a Positive Note

- Thank participants for their engagement.

- Provide contact information or additional resources for further inquiries.

Final Thoughts

Managing a Q&A session effectively in Zoom meetings requires preparation, clear communication, and strong moderation. By following these best practices, you can ensure that your sessions are interactive, informative, and engaging for all attendees.

5.3 Troubleshooting Common Issues

5.3.1 Dealing with Connection and Audio Problems

Zoom is a powerful tool for virtual communication, but like any online platform, it is susceptible to connection and audio issues. These problems can disrupt meetings, create frustration, and reduce the effectiveness of communication. In this section, we will explore common connectivity and audio problems, their causes, and step-by-step solutions to ensure a smooth Zoom experience.

1. Common Connection Issues and Their Causes

1.1 Slow or Unstable Internet Connection

One of the most frequent problems users encounter is a lagging or unstable Zoom call. This can manifest as:

- Video freezing or becoming pixelated
- Audio cutting in and out
- Delays in communication (audio/video lag)

Causes:

- Low internet speed (bandwidth issues)
- Network congestion (multiple devices using bandwidth)
- Weak Wi-Fi signal

1.2 Zoom Disconnecting or Reconnecting

Some users experience Zoom suddenly disconnecting or frequently reconnecting during meetings.

Causes:

- Internet service interruptions
- Network firewall or VPN interference

- Zoom server issues (rare but possible)

1.3 Audio Delays and Echoes

In some meetings, participants notice that audio responses are delayed or they hear an echo.

Causes:

- High network latency

- Multiple audio input sources (e.g., microphone and speaker interference)

- Poor microphone or speaker placement

2. Fixing Connection Problems

2.1 Checking Your Internet Speed

Before joining an important meeting, test your internet speed using services like **Speedtest.net** or **Fast.com**.

Recommended Minimum Speeds for Zoom:

- **1.5 Mbps** for one-on-one video calls

- **3 Mbps** for group video calls

- **5 Mbps+** for HD video meetings

If your internet speed is below these thresholds, consider:

- Upgrading your internet plan

- Limiting the number of devices using your network

- Using an Ethernet cable instead of Wi-Fi

2.2 Improving Wi-Fi Connection Stability

A weak Wi-Fi signal can cause Zoom issues. Here are some ways to strengthen your connection:

- **Move closer to the router** – The further you are, the weaker the signal.

- **Use a wired Ethernet connection** – More stable than Wi-Fi.

- **Reduce network congestion** – Pause downloads, streaming, or large file uploads during meetings.

- **Restart your router** – Sometimes, a simple restart can resolve temporary network issues.

2.3 Adjusting Zoom Video and Audio Quality Settings

If your internet connection is slow, lower the bandwidth demand by adjusting Zoom settings:

- Turn **off HD video** (Settings → Video → Uncheck "Enable HD")

- Disable **video filters and virtual backgrounds**

- Turn off **"Enable Hardware Acceleration"** under Advanced settings

---

3. Fixing Audio Issues

3.1 No Sound or Microphone Not Working

If you or a participant cannot hear audio or the microphone isn't working, check these steps:

Solution:

1. **Ensure the correct microphone is selected:**
   - Click on the **microphone icon** in Zoom
   - Select the correct input device under **Audio Settings**

2. **Test your microphone in Zoom:**
   - Go to **Settings → Audio → Test Mic**

3. **Check if the microphone is muted:**
   - Click the **Unmute** button in Zoom

4. **Restart Zoom or your computer:**
   - Restarting can reset audio configurations.

3.2 Echo or Feedback During Meetings

Echo or feedback occurs when multiple audio sources are active at the same time.

Solution:

- Ask participants to **use headphones** to prevent sound looping.

- Ensure only **one microphone and speaker** is active per device.

- If using external speakers, **reduce volume** to avoid echo.

3.3 Low or Distorted Audio Quality

If voices sound robotic, muffled, or too soft, consider these fixes:

Solution:

- Adjust **input volume** in Zoom under **Audio Settings → Microphone Volume**

- If using Bluetooth headphones, **disconnect and reconnect** them

- If using an external microphone, **check connections** and **update drivers**

---

4. Advanced Troubleshooting

4.1 Checking Zoom's Server Status

Sometimes, connection issues are not from your end but due to Zoom server outages.

- Visit **status.zoom.us** to check for server issues.

- If Zoom is down, wait for updates from their team.

4.2 Adjusting Firewall and VPN Settings

If you experience frequent disconnections, your firewall or VPN may be blocking Zoom.

- Disable VPNs while using Zoom if possible.

- Allow Zoom through your firewall under **Windows Firewall settings** or **Mac System Preferences**.

4.3 Contacting Zoom Support

If all else fails, reach out to **Zoom Support** by:

- Visiting **support.zoom.us**

- Checking the **Zoom Community Forum** for solutions

5. Preventive Measures for Future Meetings

To avoid connection and audio problems in future meetings:

- **Test your setup** before important calls (Zoom has a built-in test meeting: zoom.us/test)

- **Use a wired connection** if possible

- **Keep Zoom updated** to the latest version

By following these troubleshooting steps, you can minimize Zoom disruptions and ensure seamless virtual meetings.

5.3.2 Handling Video and Screen Freezing Issues

In a world where virtual meetings have become the norm, video and screen freezing issues can be one of the most frustrating experiences during a Zoom session. Whether you are presenting an important business proposal, teaching an online class, or catching up with loved ones, video lags and frozen screens can disrupt the flow of communication and reduce engagement.

In this section, we will explore the **common causes of video and screen freezing issues**, **step-by-step troubleshooting methods**, **preventive measures**, and **technical adjustments** to help you enjoy a seamless Zoom experience.

Common Causes of Video and Screen Freezing Issues

Before diving into solutions, it's essential to understand why video and screen freezing occurs. The following are the most common causes:

1. Weak or Unstable Internet Connection

One of the primary reasons for video freezing is an unstable internet connection. If your bandwidth is insufficient, Zoom may struggle to maintain a steady video feed, causing delays and interruptions.

2. High Network Congestion

When multiple devices on the same network consume bandwidth (e.g., streaming videos, large downloads, or other video conferencing sessions), Zoom may experience lag or freezing due to limited available bandwidth.

3. Insufficient Computer Processing Power

Zoom requires a decent amount of CPU and RAM to run smoothly. If your device is outdated or running too many applications simultaneously, the performance of Zoom can be negatively impacted.

4. Outdated Zoom Application or System Drivers

Running an outdated version of Zoom or using old system drivers (such as graphics drivers) can lead to compatibility issues, affecting video and screen sharing performance.

5. Background Applications Consuming Resources

Having multiple applications open, especially ones that use a lot of processing power (e.g., video editing software, multiple browser tabs, or heavy applications), can cause Zoom to freeze as your system struggles to allocate enough resources.

6. Firewall and Security Settings

Certain firewall settings or VPNs can interfere with Zoom's ability to maintain a stable connection, causing video interruptions.

7. Overloaded Zoom Servers

On rare occasions, Zoom's servers may experience high traffic, leading to performance issues.

Troubleshooting Steps to Fix Freezing Video and Screen Issues

Now that we understand the potential causes, let's go through practical solutions to fix the problem.

1. Check and Improve Your Internet Connection

- **Test Your Internet Speed**: Go to a speed test website (such as Speedtest.net) and check your download and upload speeds. Zoom recommends at least **3 Mbps upload and download speed** for HD video calls.

- **Switch to a Wired Connection**: If possible, use an **Ethernet cable** instead of Wi-Fi. A wired connection is generally more stable and faster.

- **Move Closer to the Router**: If you must use Wi-Fi, ensure that you are close to the router to minimize signal interference.

- **Limit Other Devices Using the Network**: Ask household members or colleagues to **pause downloads, streaming, or other video calls** while you are on Zoom.

- **Restart Your Modem and Router**: Unplug them, wait for 30 seconds, and plug them back in to refresh the connection.

2. Reduce Zoom's Bandwidth Usage

- **Lower Video Quality**: In the Zoom settings, navigate to **Video > Enable HD** and disable it to reduce bandwidth consumption.

- **Turn Off Video When Not Necessary**: If freezing persists, consider turning off your video when speaking and using only audio.

- **Disable Virtual Backgrounds**: Virtual backgrounds require additional processing power and bandwidth. Try using a plain background instead.

- **Limit Screen Sharing Quality**: When sharing your screen, **opt for "Optimize for video clip" only if necessary** to reduce strain on your connection.

3. Optimize Your Device's Performance

- **Close Unnecessary Applications**: Open **Task Manager (Windows)** or **Activity Monitor (Mac)** and close apps that are consuming too much CPU or memory.

- **Update Your Operating System**: Make sure Windows or macOS is updated to the latest version.

- **Update Graphics and Network Drivers**: Keeping your drivers updated ensures smoother video performance.

- **Use a Device with Better Hardware**: If possible, switch to a computer with a **faster processor (Intel i5 or higher)** and at least **8GB RAM** for a smoother Zoom experience.

4. Keep Zoom and Other Software Updated

- **Check for Zoom Updates**: Open Zoom, go to **Settings > Check for Updates**, and install any available updates.

- **Update Web Browser**: If using Zoom via a web browser, ensure that your browser (Chrome, Firefox, Edge) is up to date.

- **Ensure Other Communication Apps are Updated**: Apps like Microsoft Teams or Skype can interfere with Zoom if outdated.

5. Adjust Zoom Video Settings for Better Stability

- **Disable Hardware Acceleration**:
    - Open Zoom **Settings**
    - Go to **Video > Advanced**
    - Disable "Use hardware acceleration for receiving video"

- **Adjust Video Frame Rate**:
    - Under **Video Settings**, lower the frame rate if Zoom is freezing frequently.

6. Check Firewall, VPN, and Security Settings

- **Temporarily Disable VPN**: VPNs can slow down Zoom. Disconnect it and check if the issue improves.

- **Adjust Firewall Settings**: If you are using Zoom in an office environment, contact your IT department to whitelist Zoom's servers.

- **Try a Different Network**: If possible, switch to another network (e.g., mobile hotspot) to see if the issue persists.

7. Restart Zoom and Your Device

If all else fails, a simple **restart** can help resolve temporary software glitches.

- Close Zoom completely and restart your computer before rejoining the meeting.

- If necessary, uninstall and reinstall Zoom to clear any corrupted files.

Preventive Measures to Avoid Future Freezing Issues

To prevent future disruptions in Zoom meetings, here are some best practices:

1. Schedule Regular Internet Speed Checks

Test your connection regularly to ensure stable speeds, especially before important meetings.

2. Upgrade Your Internet Plan If Necessary

If you frequently experience lag, consider upgrading to a **higher-speed broadband plan**.

3. Use a High-Quality Webcam and Audio Setup

External webcams with built-in processing (such as Logitech C920) perform better than integrated laptop cameras.

4. Set Up a Distraction-Free Workspace

Ensure your workspace has a stable connection and minimal interference.

5. Keep Your Software Updated

Regular updates to Zoom, your operating system, and network drivers can help prevent compatibility issues.

Final Thoughts

Dealing with **video and screen freezing issues** can be frustrating, but with the right **troubleshooting steps** and **preventive measures**, you can significantly **improve your Zoom experience**.

By ensuring **a stable internet connection**, **optimizing your device's performance**, **keeping Zoom updated**, and **adjusting settings for efficiency**, you can minimize disruptions and conduct seamless virtual meetings.

The key is **proactive preparation**—taking a few minutes to optimize your setup **before** an important meeting can save you from technical headaches later on.

If you continue to experience persistent freezing issues despite following these steps, it may be worth **contacting Zoom Support** or seeking assistance from your IT team.

By following these best practices, you can **enhance your Zoom experience and ensure smooth, professional, and effective virtual meetings**.

5.3.3 Fixing Zoom Crashes and Errors

Zoom is a reliable video conferencing tool, but like any software, it can sometimes crash or encounter errors. Understanding the common causes and knowing how to troubleshoot these issues can help you maintain smooth and uninterrupted meetings. In this section, we will explore the most frequent reasons Zoom crashes, how to diagnose the problem, and steps to fix these issues effectively.

Common Causes of Zoom Crashes

Zoom crashes can occur due to various reasons, including hardware limitations, network instability, software conflicts, and corrupted files. Below are some of the most common causes:

1. Insufficient System Resources

- Running Zoom on an outdated or low-performance computer can lead to crashes.
- High CPU and RAM usage from multiple applications running simultaneously can cause Zoom to freeze or shut down.

2. Network Connectivity Issues

- Weak or unstable internet connections can disrupt Zoom's performance, leading to disconnections and crashes.
- Network congestion, such as multiple users streaming videos or gaming, can overload the bandwidth.

3. Outdated or Corrupt Zoom Installation

- Using an outdated version of Zoom may cause compatibility issues with your operating system.
- A corrupted installation file can result in crashes and unexpected shutdowns.

4. Conflicts with Other Applications

- Background applications, especially those that use the camera and microphone, may interfere with Zoom.

- Security software or firewalls may block Zoom's access to the internet, leading to connection failures.

5. Hardware Acceleration and GPU Issues

- Zoom relies on hardware acceleration for smooth video processing, but on some systems, this feature may cause crashes.

- Older or incompatible graphics drivers may struggle to handle Zoom's video rendering.

6. Permission and Security Restrictions

- Some operating systems require special permissions for Zoom to function correctly.

- Antivirus software or system policies may restrict Zoom's access to essential components.

How to Diagnose the Issue

Before applying a fix, it's important to diagnose the root cause of the problem. Here are some steps to identify why Zoom is crashing:

1. **Check for Error Messages** – If Zoom crashes, it may display an error message. Take note of the error code or message for troubleshooting.

2. **Monitor CPU and RAM Usage** – Open Task Manager (Windows) or Activity Monitor (Mac) to check if Zoom is consuming too many system resources.

3. **Test Your Internet Speed** – Run an internet speed test (e.g., Speedtest.net) to see if your connection is stable and fast enough for Zoom.

4. **Check for Application Conflicts** – Close unnecessary applications running in the background, especially those using audio, video, or networking features.

5. **Review System Logs** – On Windows, check Event Viewer; on Mac, check Console logs to see if there are any system-related error reports associated with Zoom.

How to Fix Zoom Crashes and Errors

1. Restart Your Device and Zoom

A simple restart can resolve many temporary software issues.

- Close Zoom completely and reopen it.
- Restart your computer to clear any temporary glitches.
- If using a mobile device, restart it and try launching Zoom again.

2. Update Zoom to the Latest Version

Keeping Zoom updated ensures that you have the latest bug fixes and performance improvements.

- Open Zoom and go to Settings > Check for Updates.
- If an update is available, install it and restart Zoom.
- If Zoom is installed from an app store (e.g., Apple App Store, Google Play Store), update it from there.

3. Close Unnecessary Background Applications

Zoom may crash if other programs are consuming too much CPU or RAM.

- Close high-resource applications like Chrome, Photoshop, or gaming software.
- Disable unnecessary startup programs that consume resources in the background.

4. Improve Network Stability

- Use a wired Ethernet connection instead of Wi-Fi for a more stable connection.
- Restart your router and modem to refresh your internet connection.
- If using Wi-Fi, move closer to the router or switch to a less crowded frequency (5GHz instead of 2.4GHz).
- Ask others on the same network to limit high-bandwidth activities like streaming or gaming.

5. Reinstall Zoom

If Zoom continues to crash, a fresh installation may fix corrupted files.

For Windows:

1. Open Control Panel > Programs > Uninstall a Program.

2. Locate Zoom, right-click, and select Uninstall.

3. Download the latest Zoom version from the official website and reinstall it.

For Mac:

1. Open Finder > Applications.

2. Locate Zoom, drag it to the Trash, and empty the Trash.

3. Download and reinstall Zoom.

6. Adjust Zoom Video and Audio Settings

If Zoom crashes during video calls, adjusting video and audio settings may help.

- Go to Zoom Settings > Video and disable HD video to reduce system load.

- Under Audio Settings, disable Background Noise Suppression if experiencing lag or crashes.

- If using an external webcam or microphone, try switching to the internal camera and mic to see if the issue persists.

7. Update Your Graphics Drivers

Zoom uses your GPU for video processing. If your graphics drivers are outdated, Zoom may crash.

For Windows:

- Open Device Manager > Display Adapters.

- Right-click your graphics card and select Update Driver.

For Mac:

- macOS updates usually include graphics driver updates. Go to System Settings > Software Update to check for updates.

8. Disable Hardware Acceleration

Disabling hardware acceleration may help if your device struggles with Zoom's video rendering.

- Open Zoom and go to Settings > Video.

- Scroll down and disable Use hardware acceleration for video processing.

- Restart Zoom and check if the issue persists.

9. Allow Zoom Through Firewall and Antivirus

Security software may block Zoom's network access.

- Go to Firewall & Network Protection settings and allow Zoom through.

- If using third-party antivirus software, add Zoom as an exception.

10. Check for System Updates

Your operating system should be up to date to ensure compatibility with Zoom.

For Windows:

- Go to Settings > Windows Update and install any pending updates.

For Mac:

- Go to System Settings > Software Update and update macOS.

Final Troubleshooting Steps

If none of the above solutions work, consider these final steps:

- Try using Zoom on a different device to see if the issue is system-related.

- Contact Zoom Support (support.zoom.us) for professional assistance.

- Use Zoom's Web Client instead of the desktop app to see if the issue persists.

Conclusion

Zoom is a powerful tool for communication, but crashes and errors can be frustrating. By following the troubleshooting steps outlined above, you can minimize disruptions and ensure a smoother meeting experience. Regular maintenance, keeping Zoom updated, and optimizing system resources will help you avoid future issues and make the most out of your virtual meetings.

CHAPTER VI
Zoom for Different Use Cases

6.1 Zoom for Business and Team Collaboration

6.1.1 Hosting Webinars and Large Meetings

Introduction

Zoom is a powerful platform that allows users to host large-scale meetings and webinars efficiently. Whether you are organizing a company-wide town hall, a professional conference, or an online training session, Zoom offers tools and features designed to engage a large audience, manage participants effectively, and ensure smooth communication.

This section will guide you through how to host webinars and large meetings on Zoom, covering:

- The difference between webinars and large meetings

- How to schedule and configure a Zoom webinar

- Essential engagement features to keep your audience involved

- Best practices for managing attendees and panelists

- Troubleshooting common issues when handling large audiences

By the end of this section, you will be equipped with the knowledge to run professional and successful large-scale events on Zoom.

Webinars vs. Large Meetings: Key Differences

Before diving into the setup, it's important to understand the key differences between Zoom Webinars and Zoom Large Meetings.

Feature	Zoom Webinars	Zoom Large Meetings
Audience Type	Viewers (Attendees)	Active Participants
Interactivity	Limited (Q&A, Polls, Chat)	High (Audio, Video, Chat)
Panelists vs. Participants	Panelists & Attendees	All Participants
Video Sharing	Only Panelists	Everyone
Best For	Webinars, Conferences, Public Events	Team Meetings, Workshops, Group Discussions

- Webinars: Best for one-to-many communication, where a host and panelists present while attendees mostly listen and engage through Q&A and chat.

- Large Meetings: Best for interactive discussions, where everyone can turn on their mic and video, similar to a regular Zoom meeting but with an extended capacity.

Depending on your event's purpose, choosing the right format will help you ensure a smooth and effective experience.

How to Schedule a Zoom Webinar or Large Meeting

Step 1: Upgrade Your Zoom Plan

To host webinars or large meetings, you need to purchase an add-on:

- Webinar Add-On: Allows hosting 100 to 10,000 attendees.

- Large Meeting Add-On: Expands meeting capacity to 500 or 1,000 participants.

You can purchase these add-ons from Zoom's billing page under "Plans & Pricing."

Step 2: Schedule Your Event

1. Sign in to Zoom and go to the Webinar or Meetings tab.

2. Click "Schedule a Webinar" or "Schedule a Meeting" (for large meetings).

3. Fill in details:

    o   Title & Description: Make it clear and engaging.

    o   Date & Time: Consider different time zones.

    o   Registration: Enable if you need attendee details.

    o   Panelists or Co-hosts: Add speakers or moderators.

Step 3: Configure Security & Access Settings

- Passcodes & Waiting Rooms: Prevent unwanted guests.

- Registration Approval: Approve attendees manually if needed.

- Mute Participants on Entry: Avoid disruptions.

Step 4: Set Up Engagement Tools

Enable:

- Q&A Panel (Webinars) for structured audience questions.

- Polls & Surveys for instant feedback.

- Chat Moderation to prevent spam.

Once configured, click "Save" and send the invitation link to participants.

Managing Attendees and Panelists

In large meetings and webinars, **effective audience management** is crucial.

Roles and Permissions

- **Host**: The primary controller of the event.

- **Co-hosts**: Assist in managing the meeting.

- **Panelists (Webinars only)**: Presenters with audio/video access.

- **Attendees**: Passive listeners (Webinars) or active participants (Meetings).

Best Practices for Managing Attendees

1. **Enable Waiting Room**: Allows manual approval of attendees.

2. **Use Spotlight Video**: Focus on the speaker.

3. **Manage Chat & Q&A**: Assign a moderator to filter spam and answer questions.

4. **Breakout Rooms (Large Meetings only)**: Organize smaller discussions.

Enhancing Engagement in Webinars and Large Meetings

Keeping your audience engaged is **key to a successful event**.

Strategies for Engagement

✓ **Use Polls**: Gather opinions and insights.
✓ **Q&A Sessions**: Answer live questions effectively.
✓ **Live Reactions & Emojis**: Encourage participation.
✓ **Interactive Presentations**: Use screen sharing & animations.
✓ **Breakout Rooms**: Small-group discussions for engagement.

Tip: Always acknowledge audience participation and make sessions interactive!

Recording and Post-Event Follow-Up

Recording Your Session

- Go to **Settings → Recording** and enable **Cloud Recording** for easy sharing.

- Announce that the session will be recorded.

- Share the **recording link** after the event.

Post-Event Engagement

✓ **Send Follow-up Emails**: Include a thank-you message and recording.
✓ **Share Key Takeaways**: Summarize important points in a document.
✓ **Collect Feedback**: Use a survey to improve future events.

Troubleshooting Large Meetings & Webinars

Common Issues and Solutions

Issue	Cause	Solution
Audio Echo	Multiple open mics	Mute unnecessary mics
Video Lag	Weak internet	Use a wired connection
Attendees Can't Join	Incorrect link	Double-check invitation
Chat Spam	Unmoderated chat	Enable moderation

For best performance, test your setup before the event and ensure a stable internet connection.

Conclusion

Hosting large meetings and webinars on Zoom requires proper planning, engagement strategies, and technical know-how. By following the steps outlined in this section, you can effectively manage large audiences, engage attendees, and deliver impactful presentations.

Key Takeaways:

✓ Choose between Webinars vs. Large Meetings based on your needs.

✓ Set up registration, security, and engagement features properly.

✓ Manage attendees and panelists effectively for a smooth experience.

✓ Use interactive tools like polls, Q&A, and reactions to boost participation.

✓ Follow up with recordings, notes, and feedback to maintain engagement.

By mastering these techniques, you'll be able to host professional and engaging large-scale events on Zoom effortlessly.

6.1.2 Using Zoom for Remote Team Meetings

Remote work has become the new norm for many businesses worldwide, and Zoom has established itself as one of the most essential tools for virtual team collaboration. Whether your team is fully remote, hybrid, or spread across different time zones, Zoom provides powerful features that enable seamless communication, collaboration, and productivity. In this section, we will explore how to effectively use Zoom for remote team meetings, covering everything from setting up meetings, best practices for engagement, and troubleshooting common challenges.

1. Setting Up a Remote Team Meeting

Scheduling a Meeting in Advance

Proper planning is essential for remote team meetings, as team members may be working in different time zones. When scheduling a meeting on Zoom, consider the following:

- **Choose a Suitable Time:** Use scheduling tools like Google Calendar, Microsoft Outlook, or World Time Buddy to find a time that works for everyone.

- **Send Invitations in Advance:** Ensure team members receive the Zoom meeting link well ahead of time, along with the agenda.

- **Enable Recurring Meetings:** If your team meets regularly, set up a recurring Zoom meeting to streamline scheduling.

- **Integrate with Calendar Apps:** Zoom integrates with Google Calendar and Outlook, making it easy for participants to add meetings to their schedules.

Setting Meeting Access Controls

Security and accessibility are crucial in remote team meetings. Consider these settings when setting up your meeting:

- **Use a Waiting Room:** This allows the host to approve participants before they enter the meeting.

- **Require a Passcode:** Adding a passcode prevents unauthorized users from joining.

- **Restrict Screen Sharing:** Limit screen sharing to the host or designated team members to avoid distractions.

- **Enable Authentication:** Require participants to sign in with their company email before joining.

Choosing the Right Zoom Settings

Configuring your Zoom settings properly enhances the experience for remote teams:

- **Enable HD Video and Audio:** High-quality video and audio improve communication.

- **Mute Participants on Entry:** This prevents background noise at the start of the meeting.

- **Enable Automatic Recording:** If necessary, record meetings for absent members to review later.

2. Running an Effective Remote Team Meeting

Establishing a Meeting Structure

A well-structured meeting keeps discussions focused and productive. Follow these steps:

- Start with a Check-In: Ask team members how they're doing to build rapport.

- Review the Agenda: Outline the topics to be covered to keep the meeting on track.

- Assign a Timekeeper: Designate someone to monitor time and keep discussions concise.

- Summarize Key Takeaways: Recap action items at the end to ensure clarity.

Using Zoom Features for Better Engagement

Zoom offers several tools to improve interaction and participation in remote meetings:

- Breakout Rooms: Divide participants into smaller groups for discussions.

- Polls and Reactions: Use built-in polling features to gather input quickly.

- Chat Box: Encourage team members to ask questions or share links during discussions.

- Virtual Backgrounds and Filters: Allow employees to personalize their experience while maintaining professionalism.

Encouraging Participation in Virtual Meetings

One common challenge in remote meetings is passive participation. Here's how to boost engagement:

- Rotate Meeting Roles: Assign different team members to lead discussions each week.

- Use Video Whenever Possible: Seeing facial expressions improves communication.

- Encourage Open Dialogue: Create a safe space for employees to share ideas and feedback.

- Limit Meeting Length: Keep meetings between 30 to 60 minutes to avoid fatigue.

3. Overcoming Challenges in Remote Team Meetings

Dealing with Technical Issues

Technical difficulties can disrupt remote meetings. Here's how to prevent them:

- Test Your Connection Beforehand: Ensure a stable internet connection.

- Use a Wired Connection If Possible: Ethernet cables provide more stable connectivity than Wi-Fi.

- Check Microphone and Camera Settings: Adjust Zoom audio/video settings before joining.

- Have a Backup Plan: If Zoom fails, have an alternative platform like Google Meet or Microsoft Teams ready.

Handling Distractions and Background Noise

Remote team members may work in various environments. Here's how to minimize disruptions:

- Encourage the Use of Headphones: This helps eliminate background noise.

- Mute When Not Speaking: Participants should mute themselves when not talking.

- Use Noise-Canceling Features: Zoom's background noise suppression can help reduce unwanted sounds.

- Set Guidelines for Professionalism: Encourage employees to attend meetings from quiet spaces.

Managing Time Zone Differences

For global teams, time zone differences can be challenging. Here are some strategies:

- Rotate Meeting Times: Alternate meeting schedules to accommodate different time zones.

- Use Asynchronous Communication: Record meetings for those who cannot attend live.

- Schedule Core Hours: Establish overlapping work hours for real-time collaboration.

- Leverage Team Collaboration Tools: Use Slack, Trello, or Microsoft Teams for ongoing discussions.

4. Post-Meeting Best Practices

Sharing Meeting Notes and Recordings

Not everyone may be able to attend live. After the meeting, share:

- Meeting Minutes: Summarize key points and action items.

- Recording Links: Provide access to Zoom cloud or local recordings.

- Follow-Up Emails: Recap decisions and next steps.

Assigning and Tracking Action Items

Ensuring accountability is key in remote work. Use these methods:

- Assign Tasks Immediately: Use project management tools like Asana or Monday.com.

- Set Deadlines: Define timelines for each action item.

- Follow Up in the Next Meeting: Review progress on tasks from previous meetings.

Gathering Feedback for Improvement

Regular feedback helps refine virtual meeting strategies:

- Use Anonymous Surveys: Collect honest feedback from team members.

- Ask for Verbal Input: Open the floor for suggestions at the end of the meeting.

- Analyze Meeting Effectiveness: Check if objectives were met and make adjustments.

5. Conclusion

Using Zoom for remote team meetings can significantly enhance communication and collaboration when used effectively. By following best practices in scheduling, engagement, and post-meeting follow-ups, remote teams can stay connected, productive, and motivated.

Mastering Zoom's features will not only improve virtual meetings but also contribute to a positive and efficient remote work culture. As technology evolves, continuously exploring new Zoom functionalities will help teams adapt to the changing landscape of remote collaboration.

6.1.3 Integrating Zoom with Slack and Microsoft Teams

Collaboration tools are essential in today's digital workplace, and integrating Zoom with platforms like **Slack** and **Microsoft Teams** can significantly enhance team communication and efficiency. Both Slack and Microsoft Teams serve as central hubs for workplace conversations, file sharing, and project management, while Zoom provides a robust video conferencing solution. By integrating these tools, organizations can streamline workflows, reduce app-switching fatigue, and improve productivity.

In this section, we will explore how to set up and use Zoom with **Slack** and **Microsoft Teams**, the benefits of integration, and best practices to maximize efficiency.

Benefits of Integrating Zoom with Slack and Microsoft Teams

Integrating Zoom with Slack and Microsoft Teams provides several advantages:

1. Seamless Meeting Scheduling and Joining

- Users can schedule, start, or join Zoom meetings directly from Slack or Microsoft Teams without switching between applications.

- Meeting reminders and notifications appear in the same workspace, ensuring better attendance.

2. Improved Team Collaboration

- Teams can instantly transition from text-based conversations to real-time video discussions with a single command.

- Integration allows users to share Zoom recordings and transcripts directly within the collaboration platform.

3. Centralized Communication

- By integrating Zoom, organizations can consolidate communication tools into one ecosystem, reducing confusion and increasing efficiency.

4. Automated Workflows

- Admins can set up automated workflows, such as sending Zoom meeting reminders or integrating Zoom recordings with project management tools.

Integrating Zoom with Slack

Slack is a popular team messaging platform that allows real-time communication and file sharing. By integrating Zoom, Slack users can initiate meetings without leaving their workspace.

Step 1: Installing the Zoom App for Slack

To integrate Zoom with Slack, follow these steps:

1. Open Slack and go to the **Apps** section.

2. Search for **Zoom** in the Slack App Directory.

3. Click **Add to Slack** and grant the necessary permissions.

4. Sign in with your Zoom account to complete the integration.

Step 2: Using Zoom Commands in Slack

Once installed, users can control Zoom meetings using Slack commands:

- **/zoom** – Starts a new Zoom meeting.

- **/zoom join [meeting ID]** – Joins an existing Zoom meeting.

- **/zoom help** – Displays available Zoom commands in Slack.

Step 3: Automating Meeting Reminders in Slack

To ensure no one misses a meeting, use Slack's automation:

- Set up scheduled reminders using **Slackbot** (e.g., "Reminder: Zoom meeting at 3 PM").

- Integrate Zoom with Slack workflows to auto-send meeting links in relevant channels.

Step 4: Sharing Zoom Meeting Summaries and Recordings in Slack

After a meeting, you can automatically share recordings in Slack channels:

1. Enable **Cloud Recording** in Zoom settings.

2. Configure Zoom to send recording links to Slack after the meeting.

Integrating Zoom with Microsoft Teams

Microsoft Teams is a powerful collaboration tool that combines chat, file sharing, and video conferencing. While Teams has its own meeting feature, many organizations prefer Zoom for video calls.

Step 1: Adding Zoom to Microsoft Teams

To integrate Zoom with Microsoft Teams:

1. Open **Microsoft Teams** and go to **Apps**.

2. Search for **Zoom** and select it from the app list.

3. Click **Add** and sign in with your Zoom account.

4. Grant the necessary permissions for Zoom to work in Teams.

Step 2: Scheduling and Starting Zoom Meetings in Teams

After integration, you can use Zoom commands inside Teams:

- **@Zoom start** – Starts a new Zoom meeting.

- **@Zoom schedule [date/time]** – Schedules a Zoom meeting.

- **@Zoom help** – Displays available Zoom commands in Teams.

Step 3: Sharing Zoom Meetings in Microsoft Teams Channels

- Paste Zoom meeting links directly into Microsoft Teams chat or channels.

- Use the **Zoom tab** inside a Teams channel to keep meeting links and recordings organized.

Step 4: Using Zoom for Large Webinars in Teams

For large-scale virtual events, organizations often prefer Zoom Webinars over Microsoft Teams meetings.

- Zoom Webinars allow up to 10,000 participants.

- You can integrate Zoom Webinars with **Microsoft Teams Live Events** for seamless streaming.

Best Practices for Using Zoom with Slack and Microsoft Teams

1. Standardize Meeting Commands Across the Organization

- Train employees on Zoom commands within Slack and Teams to ensure smooth adoption.

- Create quick-reference guides for employees on how to start and schedule Zoom meetings.

2. Use Automation for Productivity

- Set up Zoom meeting reminders in Slack and Teams channels to ensure timely participation.

- Automate post-meeting actions like recording sharing and meeting summaries.

3. Secure Your Zoom Meetings

- Enable **passcodes and waiting rooms** to prevent unauthorized access.

- Use **role-based access control** to manage Zoom meeting permissions in Slack and Teams.

4. Monitor Meeting Performance

- Use Zoom's analytics dashboard to track meeting attendance and engagement.

- Leverage Slack and Teams analytics to measure how frequently Zoom meetings are used.

Conclusion

Integrating Zoom with Slack and Microsoft Teams is a game-changer for modern workplaces. It reduces friction between communication tools, allowing teams to schedule, join, and manage Zoom meetings seamlessly within their collaboration platforms.

By following the setup guides and best practices outlined in this section, businesses and educational institutions can maximize the benefits of Zoom integration. Whether for daily stand-ups, client meetings, or large-scale webinars, this integration ensures a more efficient, connected, and productive virtual environment.

6.2 Zoom for Education and Online Learning

6.2.1 Engaging Students with Interactive Features

As education continues to evolve in the digital age, Zoom has become a critical tool for online learning. However, simply conducting virtual lectures is not enough to ensure effective student engagement. Educators must leverage Zoom's interactive features to create a dynamic, engaging, and participatory learning experience. In this section, we will explore how teachers, trainers, and instructors can use Zoom's interactive tools to keep students motivated, encourage participation, and enhance learning outcomes.

1. Understanding the Importance of Student Engagement in Virtual Learning

Engagement is one of the biggest challenges in online learning. In traditional classrooms, instructors can easily gauge students' attention and understanding through body language, facial expressions, and immediate responses. However, in a virtual setting, these cues are often missing, making it crucial for educators to actively incorporate interactive elements to maintain student focus and participation.

Interactive learning leads to better comprehension, higher retention rates, and improved overall satisfaction. Research has shown that students who actively participate in discussions, group activities, and hands-on exercises perform better academically compared to those who passively consume information. Zoom provides numerous features that help bridge this gap and make virtual learning more engaging.

2. Key Interactive Features in Zoom for Engaging Students

2.1 Polls and Quizzes

Polls are an excellent way to assess student understanding, gather opinions, or initiate discussions. Educators can set up single-choice or multiple-choice polls before the class begins and launch them at key moments to keep students engaged.

- **How to Use Polls in Zoom:**

1. Go to your Zoom meeting settings and enable the **Polling** feature.

2. Before starting your class, create polls in the Zoom web portal.

3. During the session, launch a poll and allow students to respond in real time.

4. Share the results with the class to foster discussions.

To enhance engagement, consider using polls to:

-   Test prior knowledge before starting a lesson.

-   Conduct quick quizzes to reinforce learning points.

-   Gather feedback on how students are feeling about the pace of the class.

2.2 Breakout Rooms for Group Collaboration

Breakout Rooms are one of Zoom's most powerful features for engaging students. They allow educators to divide the class into smaller groups for discussions, problem-solving exercises, or collaborative projects.

-   **How to Use Breakout Rooms Effectively:**

    1. Pre-assign students to groups or assign them randomly during the session.

    2. Clearly communicate the purpose and duration of the breakout session.

    3. Provide discussion prompts or problem-solving tasks before sending students into rooms.

    4. Move between breakout rooms to check progress and offer guidance.

    5. After the session, have students present their findings to the main class.

Breakout rooms work well for peer-to-peer learning, debates, and case study discussions, making lessons more interactive and engaging.

2.3 Reactions and Non-Verbal Feedback

Since online classes can feel less personal, Zoom provides a **Reactions** feature that allows students to express themselves non-verbally. These reactions include emojis such as a thumbs-up, clapping hands, or a raised hand, which help maintain classroom interaction.

- **How to Encourage Students to Use Reactions:**
  - Ask students to give a thumbs-up if they understand a concept.
  - Use the **raise hand** feature for students who want to ask a question.
  - Encourage students to clap for a classmate's presentation.

This real-time feedback helps educators gauge student engagement levels and adjust their teaching accordingly.

2.4 Chat and Q&A for Active Participation

The **Chat** feature in Zoom allows students to engage in discussions, ask questions, and share ideas without interrupting the flow of the lecture. Educators can use chat to:

- Ask students to type quick answers to review questions.
- Share links to relevant resources.
- Conduct **peer discussions** where students respond to each other's questions.

For large classes, enabling the **Q&A** feature (in Zoom Webinar mode) can help organize student queries more effectively.

2.5 The Whiteboard Feature for Visual Learning

Zoom's **Whiteboard** feature enables real-time drawing, writing, and diagram creation, making it a great tool for:

- **Math and science lessons** where equations and diagrams need to be illustrated.
- **Brainstorming sessions** where students can add their ideas collectively.
- **Concept mapping**, helping students visualize relationships between ideas.

To use the Whiteboard:

1. Click on **Share Screen** and select **Whiteboard**.
2. Use drawing tools, text boxes, and shapes to present concepts.
3. Allow students to annotate on the whiteboard for collaborative activities.

3. Strategies to Maximize Student Engagement on Zoom

3.1 Setting Expectations and Guidelines

To encourage active participation, educators should establish clear expectations at the beginning of the course. These include:

- Requiring students to turn on their cameras whenever possible.
- Encouraging the use of chat, reactions, and verbal participation.
- Setting rules for respectful online discussions.

3.2 Encouraging Active Participation

Instead of delivering one-way lectures, educators should:

- Ask open-ended questions frequently.
- Call on students randomly to keep them engaged.
- Create **peer-led discussions**, allowing students to take turns leading conversations.

3.3 Using Multimedia and Interactive Content

To prevent Zoom fatigue, integrate different forms of content such as:

- **Videos** to illustrate key concepts.
- **Infographics** for visual explanations.
- **Gamified quizzes** using third-party tools like Kahoot or Mentimeter.

---

4. Case Study: A Successful Zoom Classroom

To illustrate the impact of interactive features, let's consider **Professor Jane**, who teaches an online psychology course. Before using Zoom's engagement tools, her students were passive and distracted.

- **Before:**
    - Lectures were one-directional with minimal student interaction.

- o   Students frequently multitasked, leading to low retention rates.

- **After Implementing Interactive Features:**

    - o   She started using **polls** to assess understanding.

    - o   Breakout rooms were used for group activities and discussions.

    - o   The whiteboard feature made abstract concepts more tangible.

As a result, class participation increased by **60%**, and student feedback improved significantly.

---

5. Conclusion: Enhancing Online Learning Through Zoom's Interactive Features

Interactive learning is key to keeping students engaged in virtual classrooms. By leveraging Zoom's powerful features—**polls, breakout rooms, reactions, chat, and the whiteboard**—educators can create an immersive and participatory learning environment.

To maximize student engagement:

1.   Utilize a mix of interactive tools to cater to different learning styles.

2.   Set clear expectations for student participation.

3.   Continuously adapt and seek feedback to improve online teaching strategies.

With thoughtful implementation, Zoom can transform virtual education into an engaging and effective experience for students worldwide.

6.2.2 Managing Virtual Classrooms

Introduction

As online education continues to grow, Zoom has become a crucial tool for educators and students. Managing a virtual classroom effectively requires more than just logging into a meeting—it involves setting up a structured environment, keeping students engaged, and addressing technical challenges. This section will guide you through the best practices for managing virtual classrooms, from setting up Zoom properly to implementing interactive teaching strategies and handling classroom discipline in an online setting.

1. Setting Up a Structured Virtual Classroom

A well-organized virtual classroom fosters engagement and minimizes disruptions. Here are the key steps to ensure your online class is set up for success:

1.1 Scheduling and Organizing Classes

Before you start teaching, schedule your Zoom classes in a structured manner:

- Use Recurring Meetings: If your class meets regularly, set up a recurring Zoom meeting with a fixed Meeting ID to maintain consistency.

- Integrate with Learning Management Systems (LMS): Platforms like Google Classroom, Moodle, or Blackboard can integrate with Zoom, making it easier for students to access sessions.

- Send Reminders and Calendar Invites: Use automated reminders and calendar invites to ensure students don't forget upcoming sessions.

1.2 Configuring Meeting Settings for a Classroom

Configuring Zoom settings correctly can make a big difference in maintaining order and security in your virtual classroom:

- Enable the Waiting Room: This allows you to control who enters the class, preventing uninvited guests from disrupting the session.

- Mute Participants Upon Entry: This reduces background noise and ensures a focused start to the lesson.

- Disable Private Chat (If Necessary): Prevent distractions by limiting private messaging between students during class time.

- Allow Only Authenticated Users: If you're teaching a specific group, require students to log in with their school email accounts.

2. Engaging Students in a Virtual Classroom

Keeping students engaged in an online setting is one of the biggest challenges of virtual teaching. Here are some strategies to make classes more interactive:

2.1 Using Zoom's Engagement Features

- Breakout Rooms: Divide students into small groups for discussions, group work, or peer reviews. Assigning a moderator in each group helps keep discussions on track.

- Polls and Quizzes: Use Zoom's polling feature to ask quick questions, conduct knowledge checks, or gauge opinions.

- Reactions and Emoji Feedback: Encourage students to use the thumbs-up or clapping emoji to show participation without interrupting the speaker.

2.2 Encouraging Student Participation

- Use the Raise Hand Feature: Teach students to use the "Raise Hand" button when they want to speak, creating an orderly discussion flow.

- Call on Students by Name: Addressing students directly encourages participation and engagement.

- Incorporate Multimedia: Use videos, slideshows, and whiteboard tools to make lessons visually stimulating.

2.3 Assigning Roles to Students

Assigning responsibilities to students can enhance engagement and help maintain structure:

- Discussion Leaders: Assign students to lead certain discussions.

- Note-Takers: Have one or more students summarize key points in the Zoom chat or on a shared document.

- Tech Support Assistants: If you have a tech-savvy student, they can help classmates troubleshoot minor technical issues.

3. Maintaining Classroom Discipline in a Virtual Setting

Discipline in a virtual classroom differs from a physical one. Teachers need to be proactive in setting expectations and managing disruptions.

3.1 Setting Clear Expectations

- Establish Virtual Classroom Rules: Define rules such as keeping cameras on, muting when not speaking, and using the chat feature appropriately.

- Start with a Class Contract: Have students agree to basic etiquette rules at the beginning of the course.

3.2 Managing Disruptions and Misbehavior

- Use the "Mute All" Feature: If students talk over each other or create noise, mute all participants to regain control.

- Turn Off Chat if Necessary: If students misuse the chat for off-topic discussions, disable the feature temporarily.

- Remove Disruptive Students: If someone continues to cause issues, you can remove them from the session.

3.3 Encouraging a Respectful Online Environment

- Promote a Positive Atmosphere: Encourage respect and kindness in discussions.

- Model Professionalism: The way you interact sets the tone for the class.

4. Handling Technical Challenges in Virtual Classrooms

4.1 Preparing for Common Issues

- Connectivity Problems: Encourage students to check their internet connection before class. Have a backup plan, such as an alternative way to access class materials.

- Audio and Video Issues: Teach students how to check their microphone and camera settings in Zoom.

- Zoom Crashes: If Zoom crashes, have a protocol in place for students to reconnect.

4.2 Recording Lessons for Accessibility

- Enable Automatic Recording: This ensures students who miss class can catch up.

- Share Recorded Sessions Securely: Upload recordings to a secure platform like Google Drive or your LMS.

4.3 Providing Alternative Learning Options

Not all students have stable internet access. Provide:

- Offline Resources: PDFs, recorded lectures, and slides.

- Discussion Boards: Encourage continued learning through LMS discussion forums.

Conclusion

Managing a virtual classroom on Zoom requires a combination of structured planning, engaging teaching strategies, and effective classroom management. By leveraging Zoom's features, setting clear expectations, and being prepared for technical challenges, educators can create a dynamic and effective online learning environment.

6.2.3 Recording and Sharing Lectures

With the rise of online education and remote learning, Zoom has become an essential tool for educators and students alike. One of Zoom's most valuable features is the ability to record lectures, allowing students to revisit lessons, review complex topics, and learn at their own pace. This section will guide you through the process of recording lectures, managing recordings, and sharing them effectively with students.

1. Understanding Zoom Recording Options

Before recording a lecture, it is important to understand the two types of Zoom recordings available:

Local Recording vs. Cloud Recording

Zoom provides two primary recording options:

- **Local Recording:** This saves the recorded file directly to your computer. It is available for both free and paid Zoom accounts and is best suited for individual educators who prefer to store and manage files on their own devices.

- **Cloud Recording:** This option saves recordings directly to Zoom's cloud storage and is available only for paid Zoom accounts. Cloud recordings are easily shareable via links, making them ideal for schools, universities, and large educational institutions.

Choosing the Right Recording Option

When deciding between local and cloud recording, consider the following factors:

- **Storage Capacity:** If your device has limited storage, cloud recording is a better option.

- **Accessibility:** Cloud recordings allow students to access lectures from anywhere without downloading large files.

- **Security and Privacy:** Cloud storage may have additional security features like password protection and access restrictions.

2. How to Record a Lecture in Zoom

Setting Up Your Lecture for Recording

Before starting your lecture, make sure you:

- Choose a quiet environment to minimize background noise.

- Use a high-quality microphone for clear audio.

- Check your internet connection to avoid disruptions.

- Prepare your materials (slides, videos, notes) in advance.

Starting a Recording

Follow these steps to start recording your lecture:

1. **Start or Schedule Your Zoom Meeting:** Launch Zoom and either start an instant meeting or schedule a session in advance.

2. **Enable Recording:** Click on the **"Record"** button at the bottom of the Zoom toolbar.

3. **Choose the Recording Type:** If you have a paid account, select either **"Record on this Computer"** (for local storage) or **"Record to the Cloud"** (for cloud storage).

4. **Ensure All Audio and Video Are Captured:**

   o   Make sure your microphone and camera are working properly.

   o   If using PowerPoint, whiteboards, or shared screens, ensure they are visible in the recording.

5. **Use the Pause and Stop Functions:** You can pause the recording when needed and resume later. When the lecture ends, click **"Stop Recording."**

---

3. Managing and Editing Zoom Recordings

After recording, you may want to edit the lecture to remove unnecessary sections or enhance the video quality.

Locating Your Recording

- **For Local Recordings:**

   o   After the meeting ends, Zoom will automatically process and save the recording to your computer.

   o   The default location is usually in the **Documents > Zoom** folder.

- **For Cloud Recordings:**

   o   Go to **zoom.us > My Account > Recordings.**

   o   You can view, download, or share your recorded lecture.

Editing the Recording

While Zoom does not offer built-in video editing tools, you can use third-party software such as:

- **Camtasia** – A user-friendly editor for trimming and enhancing recordings.

- **Adobe Premiere Pro** – For advanced video editing.

- **iMovie (Mac) or Windows Video Editor** – Basic tools for trimming and adding subtitles.

Common edits you might make:

- **Removing unnecessary sections** (e.g., pauses, technical difficulties).

- **Adding captions or subtitles** for accessibility.

- **Enhancing audio** by reducing background noise.

4. Sharing Your Recorded Lecture

Once the recording is ready, you need to share it effectively with students.

Sharing Local Recordings

If you recorded the lecture locally, you can upload it to:

- Google Drive or OneDrive: Generate a shareable link and distribute it via email or an LMS (Learning Management System).

- YouTube (Unlisted or Private): Uploading to YouTube allows students to stream the lecture without downloading large files.

- University/School Platforms: Many institutions provide their own cloud storage or LMS like Moodle, Blackboard, or Canvas.

Sharing Cloud Recordings

If you recorded the lecture to Zoom's cloud, follow these steps:

1. Go to **zoom.us > My Account > Recordings.**

2. Click on the recorded lecture and select **"Share"**.

3. Adjust settings such as:

   o Allowing downloads.

   o Adding a password for security.

   o Setting an expiration date for access.

4. Copy the shareable link and send it to students.

Using Learning Management Systems (LMS)

For formal education settings, uploading recordings to an LMS offers additional features such as:

- Tracking student engagement (who watched the video and for how long).

- Adding timestamps and notes for easy navigation.

- Integrating quizzes and assignments related to the lecture content.

5. Best Practices for Recording and Sharing Zoom Lectures

To maximize the effectiveness of recorded lectures, follow these best practices:

5.1 Improving Video and Audio Quality

- Use a high-resolution webcam for better clarity.

- Ensure good lighting to enhance visibility.

- Use a noise-canceling microphone to reduce background noise.

- Speak clearly and slowly for better comprehension.

5.2 Making Lectures Interactive

Even though recorded lectures are one-way communication, you can add interactive elements:

- Insert breaks for reflection where students can pause and think.

- Include pre-recorded Q&A sessions at the end.

- Direct students to discussion forums where they can ask follow-up questions.

5.3 Ensuring Accessibility

- Add subtitles and closed captions to aid non-native speakers and students with hearing impairments.

- Provide written transcripts for quick reference.

- Optimize recordings for mobile viewing, as many students watch lectures on their phones.

6. Conclusion

Recording and sharing lectures on Zoom is a powerful tool for educators, offering flexibility for students and improving learning outcomes. By using the right recording settings, editing tools, and sharing methods, educators can create high-quality lecture videos that enhance student engagement.

Whether you are teaching in a university, tutoring online, or conducting corporate training, implementing best practices for Zoom recordings ensures that your lectures are accessible, clear, and effective for all learners.

6.3 Zoom for Personal Use and Social Gatherings

6.3.1 Virtual Family Meetings and Celebrations

Introduction

In today's digital world, staying connected with loved ones has never been easier, thanks to video conferencing tools like Zoom. Whether you're catching up with family members across the country, celebrating a birthday, or organizing a virtual holiday gathering, Zoom offers a range of features to help make these moments special. This section will guide you through the best practices for setting up and hosting virtual family meetings and celebrations on Zoom, ensuring a seamless and enjoyable experience for everyone involved.

1. Planning a Virtual Family Meeting or Celebration

Deciding the Purpose of the Gathering

Before setting up your Zoom meeting, determine the purpose of the virtual event. Different types of family gatherings may require different Zoom settings and features. Here are some common use cases:

- Casual Catch-Ups – A simple meeting where family members check in and chat.

- Birthday Parties – Includes games, singing, and virtual cake-cutting ceremonies.

- Holidays & Festivities – Celebrating Christmas, Thanksgiving, Hanukkah, Lunar New Year, or any cultural or religious event.

- Reunions – A large family gathering where multiple generations join from different locations.

- Memorial Services – Honoring a loved one who has passed away, allowing family members to come together in remembrance.

Choosing the Right Date and Time

Coordinating schedules for multiple family members in different time zones can be challenging. Consider the following when selecting the best time for the meeting:

- Use tools like World Time Buddy to find a time that accommodates everyone.

- Poll family members using a group chat or a scheduling tool like Doodle to find the most suitable time.

- Consider hosting two sessions if the family is spread across vastly different time zones.

Sending Invitations and Reminders

Once the date and time are confirmed, send out invitations via email, WhatsApp, or family group chats. Here's how you can effectively invite family members:

- Use Zoom's Scheduling Feature to create a meeting link in advance.

- Integrate with Google Calendar or Outlook to send automatic reminders.

- Provide clear instructions on how to join the meeting, especially for older family members who may not be tech-savvy.

2. Setting Up a Zoom Meeting for Family Gatherings

Choosing the Right Zoom Plan

For smaller gatherings, Zoom's free plan (40-minute limit for group meetings) may be sufficient. However, if you're planning a longer event, consider upgrading to Zoom Pro, which allows unlimited meeting duration and more participants.

Configuring Zoom Settings

To create a smooth experience, adjust your Zoom settings before the event:

- Enable Gallery View – Allows everyone to see multiple family members at once.

- Turn On Automatic Recording – Useful for preserving memories.

- Enable Virtual Backgrounds – Fun for themed events or seasonal celebrations.

- Set Up a Waiting Room – Helps the host manage who joins the meeting.

- Allow Co-Hosts – Assign family members as co-hosts to help manage the event.

3. Making Virtual Gatherings More Engaging

Icebreaker Activities and Introductions

If the family meeting includes members who haven't spoken in a while, start with an icebreaker to make everyone feel comfortable. Some ideas include:

- "Two Truths and a Lie" – Each person states three things about themselves, and others guess the false one.
- Favorite Family Memory – Each person shares a cherished memory about the family.
- Quick Catch-Up – Everyone shares one positive update from their life.

Playing Virtual Games

Adding interactive games can make the gathering more enjoyable. Some popular options include:

- Trivia Night – Use Kahoot! or Zoom's poll feature to create family trivia questions.
- Pictionary – Use Zoom's Whiteboard feature to play this classic drawing game.
- Charades – Family members act out words while others guess.
- Bingo – Send digital Bingo cards to participants and play together.

Virtual Party Elements

For special celebrations like birthdays or anniversaries, consider adding:

- Virtual Cake Cutting – Ask the birthday person to cut a cake on camera while others do the same at home.
- Photo Slideshow – Share a screen with memorable family photos.
- Live Music or Karaoke – Let a family member play an instrument, or use a karaoke app for sing-alongs.

4. Overcoming Common Challenges

Helping Less Tech-Savvy Family Members

Not all family members are comfortable with technology. Here's how to assist them:

- Provide a simple **step-by-step guide** on how to join a Zoom meeting.

- Offer a **test run** before the main event.

- Assign a tech-savvy **family member as a helper** to assist those who need guidance.

Managing Large Family Reunions

If you have a large family (50+ participants), Zoom meetings can become chaotic. Try these solutions:

- **Use Breakout Rooms** – Divide the family into smaller groups for more meaningful conversations.

- **Assign a Moderator** – Have someone manage who speaks and keep the event organized.

- **Mute All Participants on Entry** – Reduces background noise and confusion.

Avoiding Zoom Fatigue

Virtual gatherings can be tiring, so keep these points in mind:

- **Limit Meeting Length** – Keep it under 90 minutes if possible.

- **Schedule Short Breaks** – If the gathering is long, allow time for people to step away.

- **Encourage Participation** – Keep family members engaged with activities.

5. Preserving Memories from Virtual Gatherings

Recording and Sharing the Event

Zoom allows you to record meetings so family members who missed the event can watch later.

- Store recordings in Google Drive, OneDrive, or Dropbox for easy sharing.
- Edit highlights into a short video montage using free editing tools like iMovie or CapCut.

Creating a Digital Family Album

After the event, compile screenshots, chat messages, and shared photos into a family album.

- Use Canva or Google Photos to create a digital scrapbook.
- Share it via Facebook Groups, WhatsApp, or email newsletters.

Planning the Next Virtual Gathering

To keep family connections strong:

- Set a regular schedule for virtual meetings (monthly, quarterly, etc.).
- Rotate the host so different family members take turns planning the events.
- Keep an open family WhatsApp or Discord group to share updates between meetings.

Conclusion

Virtual family meetings and celebrations are a great way to stay connected with loved ones, no matter where they are in the world. With the right planning, engaging activities, and thoughtful use of Zoom's features, these gatherings can be just as meaningful and enjoyable as in-person events. Whether it's a casual check-in or a large family reunion, Zoom provides an accessible and interactive way to bring families together.

By implementing the tips and strategies in this guide, you'll be able to host unforgettable virtual events that strengthen family bonds and create lasting memories. So, schedule your next family Zoom call and start celebrating together—virtually!

6.3.2 Hosting Online Events and Parties

Introduction

Zoom is not just a tool for business meetings or online learning—it has also become a popular platform for hosting virtual social gatherings, celebrations, and parties. Whether you're planning a birthday party, a holiday celebration, or a casual get-together with friends and family, Zoom provides a versatile and interactive space for people to connect, even when they are miles apart.

Hosting an online event or party requires careful planning to ensure that the experience is engaging, fun, and smooth for all participants. From choosing the right Zoom settings to incorporating interactive elements, this section will guide you through the process of organizing and running a successful virtual party.

Planning Your Online Event or Party

Just like in-person events, virtual parties require **planning and preparation** to make them enjoyable for guests. Below are some key aspects to consider:

1. Choosing the Type of Event

Before you start setting up your Zoom party, decide on the type of event you want to host. Some common virtual event ideas include:

- Birthday parties – Invite friends and family for a fun-filled celebration with games, music, and virtual cake-cutting.

- Holiday gatherings – Celebrate holidays like Christmas, Thanksgiving, or New Year's Eve with virtual cheers, activities, and festive decorations.

- Game nights – Host a trivia night, a virtual escape room, or classic party games to keep your guests entertained.

- Movie watch parties – Use screen sharing and streaming services to watch movies together in sync.

- Karaoke nights – Encourage guests to showcase their singing talents using Zoom's audio-sharing features.

- Themed parties – Organize a costume party, a virtual cocktail night, or a talent show for a unique experience.

2. Setting the Date and Time

Since Zoom allows participants to join from different locations, consider the following:

- Choose a time that is convenient for most guests, especially if they are in different time zones.

- Use tools like Google Calendar to check availability.

- If needed, schedule multiple sessions to accommodate different groups.

3. Creating and Sending Invitations

Once the details are set, create an invitation with:

- The Zoom meeting link and passcode (if applicable).

- The date and time (including time zone information).

- A short description of the event.

- Dress code or theme details (if applicable).

- Instructions on how to join (especially for those unfamiliar with Zoom).

You can send invitations via **email, social media, or messaging apps**, or even create an event page on platforms like Facebook or Eventbrite.

Setting Up Your Zoom Event

1. Choosing the Right Zoom Settings

To ensure a smooth experience, adjust the following Zoom settings:

- Enable waiting rooms – This helps manage when guests enter the event and prevents unwanted interruptions.

- Set up breakout rooms – If your event involves small group activities, breakout rooms allow participants to interact in smaller groups.

- Enable screen sharing – If you or your guests plan to share videos, presentations, or games, make sure screen sharing is enabled.

- Adjust audio and video settings – Encourage participants to turn on their cameras for better engagement, and ensure that background noise is minimized.

- Use virtual backgrounds – Set a festive or themed virtual background to add to the party atmosphere.

2. Assigning Co-Hosts

For larger events, having a co-host can help with:

- Managing participants and muting/unmuting microphones.

- Monitoring the chat for questions or technical issues.

- Handling breakout rooms and transitions between activities.

3. Preparing Fun Zoom Features

Zoom offers built-in features that can make your party more interactive:

- Polls and surveys – Use polls to engage guests with fun questions or icebreakers.

- Reactions and emojis – Encourage guests to use reactions (like clapping or heart emojis) to express themselves.

- Virtual hand-raising – Useful for games, Q&A sessions, or performances.

- Filters and effects – Zoom's video filters can add a fun twist, such as virtual sunglasses or party hats.

Hosting a Fun and Engaging Party

1. Icebreakers and Introductions

Start your event with an **icebreaker** to make everyone feel comfortable. Some ideas include:

- **"Two Truths and a Lie"** – Each person shares two true facts and one false fact about themselves, and others guess which one is false.

- **Virtual scavenger hunt** – Ask guests to find household items within a time limit.

- **Storytelling chain** – One person starts a story, and each participant adds a sentence.

2. Interactive Activities and Games

To keep guests engaged, incorporate fun activities:

- **Trivia games** – Use Zoom's polling feature or external quiz platforms like Kahoot!

- **Virtual escape rooms** – Participate in online escape room experiences that challenge guests to solve puzzles together.

- **Bingo** – Create custom bingo cards related to the event theme.

- **Pictionary** – Use the Zoom whiteboard feature to play drawing and guessing games.

3. Playing Music and Dancing

- **Use Spotify or YouTube playlists** and share your computer audio so everyone can enjoy the music.

- **Host a dance-off** and encourage guests to show off their moves.

4. Screen Sharing for Movie Nights

- Use **Netflix Party (Teleparty)** or **screen sharing** to watch movies together.

- Remind participants to **check their internet connection** for the best streaming experience.

5. Ending the Event on a High Note

- **Take a group screenshot** as a memory of the event.

- **Thank everyone for attending** and encourage them to share feedback.

- **Provide next steps** if it's a recurring event (e.g., "Join us next month for another fun night!").

Troubleshooting Common Issues

Even with careful planning, technical issues may arise. Here's how to handle them:

1. Audio or Video Problems

- Ask participants to check their microphone and camera settings.
- If there's background noise, mute guests who aren't speaking.
- Encourage participants to use headphones for better audio quality.

2. Lag and Connection Issues

- If guests experience lag, suggest they turn off their video to improve bandwidth.
- Ensure that the host has a strong internet connection to prevent disconnections.

3. Screen Sharing Issues

- If guests can't share their screen, check that screen sharing permissions are enabled in Zoom settings.

Conclusion

Hosting a virtual party on Zoom can be an exciting and memorable experience with the right planning and execution. By choosing a fun theme, setting up engaging activities, and utilizing Zoom's interactive features, you can create a lively event that brings people together, no matter where they are.

With a little creativity and preparation, Zoom can become the perfect virtual venue for celebrations, game nights, movie parties, and more. So go ahead—plan your next virtual event and make it one to remember!

6.3.3 Using Zoom for Fitness and Hobby Groups

In recent years, Zoom has become more than just a tool for business meetings and online learning—it has also become a platform for social interactions, fitness classes, and hobby groups. Whether you want to attend a virtual yoga session, join a book club, or participate in an online art workshop, Zoom provides a convenient and interactive way to connect with like-minded people from anywhere in the world.

This section explores how Zoom can be effectively used for fitness classes and hobby groups, covering key aspects such as setting up meetings, engaging participants, using interactive features, and ensuring a smooth virtual experience.

Why Use Zoom for Fitness and Hobby Groups?

Accessibility and Convenience

One of the biggest advantages of using Zoom for fitness and hobby groups is accessibility. Participants can join sessions from the comfort of their own homes, eliminating the need for travel and making it easier to fit activities into their daily schedules. Whether you are a fitness instructor, a hobbyist, or someone looking for a new way to stay connected, Zoom provides a flexible and user-friendly solution.

Global Reach and Community Building

Zoom allows people from different locations to come together and share common interests. A fitness instructor in New York can train clients in London, or a knitting enthusiast in Tokyo can join a virtual club with members from Canada. This global reach fosters a sense of community, enabling participants to learn from different cultures and perspectives.

Cost-Effectiveness

For many, using Zoom for fitness and hobby groups is a cost-effective alternative to traditional in-person classes. Instructors can save on rental fees for physical spaces, and participants can access high-quality sessions at a lower cost. Hobby groups, such as book clubs or language exchange meetups, can also operate without any expenses related to venue bookings.

Setting Up a Zoom Session for Fitness and Hobby Groups

Choosing the Right Zoom Plan

Before setting up a session, it's important to determine whether the free Zoom plan is sufficient or if a paid plan is needed.

- **Zoom Basic (Free Plan)**:
    - 40-minute limit for group meetings
    - Up to 100 participants
    - Suitable for small hobby groups with short sessions

- **Zoom Pro or Business Plans**:
    - Longer meeting durations
    - More participants allowed
    - Useful for professional fitness instructors and large hobby groups

Scheduling and Managing Sessions

To create a successful fitness or hobby group session, follow these steps:

1. **Plan the Session**:
    - Define the session's objectives (e.g., a 30-minute HIIT workout or a weekly book discussion).
    - Decide on the frequency (one-time event, weekly, or daily).
    - Choose the best time based on participants' availability.

2. **Schedule the Meeting**:
    - Go to **Zoom → Schedule a Meeting**.
    - Set the date, time, and duration.
    - Enable the **waiting room** feature for security.

3. **Share the Meeting Link**:

- Send invites via email, social media, or group chat apps like WhatsApp or Discord.
- Use a calendar integration to remind participants.

4. **Prepare the Virtual Space**:

- Ensure proper lighting and camera angles, especially for fitness classes.
- Test the microphone and speaker settings before starting.

Engaging Participants in Virtual Fitness and Hobby Sessions

Making Sessions Interactive

Virtual sessions can sometimes feel less engaging than in-person activities, but Zoom offers several features to keep participants involved:

- **Breakout Rooms**:
  - Useful for dividing participants into smaller discussion groups for hobbies like language exchange or chess tournaments.

- **Polls and Reactions**:
  - Instructors can ask quick questions via Zoom polls to gauge participants' preferences.
  - Reactions (e.g., thumbs up, clapping emoji) provide real-time feedback.

- **Screen Sharing and Whiteboard**:
  - Useful for explaining complex exercises in fitness sessions.
  - Ideal for hobby groups such as drawing workshops or coding classes.

Encouraging Participation and Consistency

Maintaining an active and engaged community is essential for the success of virtual fitness and hobby groups. Some strategies include:

- **Setting Challenges**:

- o Fitness instructors can introduce monthly fitness challenges to motivate members.

- o Hobby groups can set goals (e.g., "Read one book per month" for a book club).

- **Using Social Media for Engagement**:

  - o Create a private Facebook group or WhatsApp chat for discussions outside of Zoom.

  - o Share progress updates and success stories.

- **Recognizing Achievements**:

  - o Shoutouts and virtual badges can keep members motivated.

Overcoming Challenges in Virtual Fitness and Hobby Groups

Technical Difficulties

Like any online platform, Zoom can present technical challenges. Here are some common issues and solutions:

- **Lag and Connectivity Issues**:

  - o Ask participants to close unnecessary applications to improve Zoom performance.

  - o Suggest using a wired internet connection for more stability.

- **Audio Problems**:

  - o Encourage participants to use headphones to reduce background noise.

  - o Use Zoom's "Mute All" feature to eliminate distractions during fitness classes.

- **Camera and Lighting Issues**:

  - o Recommend good lighting setups to improve visibility.

    o   Use virtual backgrounds if necessary.

Maintaining Engagement in a Virtual Environment

Keeping people engaged in a virtual setting can be challenging, especially for long-term activities. Consider the following:

- **Rotating Leadership**:
  - Assign different members to lead sessions occasionally to bring fresh energy.

- **Gamification**:
  - Introduce reward systems (e.g., prizes for most active participants).

- **Regular Feedback**:
  - Conduct surveys to understand what participants enjoy and what can be improved.

Case Studies: Real-Life Examples of Zoom in Action

Virtual Yoga and Meditation Classes

Many yoga instructors have successfully transitioned their classes online using Zoom. By utilizing breakout rooms, they offer personalized guidance, while screen sharing allows them to showcase posture corrections.

Book Clubs and Creative Writing Groups

Book clubs use Zoom to host weekly discussions, with features like "Raise Hand" for turn-taking and breakout rooms for small group discussions. Creative writing groups also use the platform for feedback sessions and virtual writing workshops.

Gaming and Esports Communities

Some gaming communities use Zoom for strategy discussions and team coordination. With screen sharing, players can analyze past games and develop new tactics together.

Conclusion

Zoom has revolutionized the way people engage in fitness and hobby activities, making it easier than ever to connect with others regardless of location. Whether you're an instructor, a hobbyist, or simply someone looking to stay active, Zoom provides the tools needed to create engaging and interactive sessions. By leveraging features like screen sharing, breakout rooms, and interactive polls, organizers can ensure participants remain motivated and connected.

As technology continues to evolve, virtual fitness and hobby groups will likely become even more popular. By adopting best practices and continuously exploring new ways to enhance engagement, individuals and communities can maximize the benefits of online interactions.

Conclusion

7.1 Recap of Key Zoom Features

As we reach the conclusion of this guide, it's essential to take a step back and review the key features that make Zoom such a powerful tool for virtual communication. Whether you use Zoom for business meetings, educational purposes, or personal gatherings, mastering its core functionalities can greatly enhance your experience. This section will summarize the essential tools and advanced features that contribute to effective and productive Zoom meetings.

7.1.1 Essential Tools for Effective Meetings

To ensure that your Zoom meetings run smoothly and efficiently, you need to utilize the right tools. These essential features help hosts and participants communicate effectively, collaborate seamlessly, and maintain a professional meeting environment. Let's explore the fundamental tools that are critical for successful Zoom meetings.

1. Scheduling and Managing Meetings

One of the most important aspects of using Zoom is the ability to schedule and manage meetings efficiently. The **Scheduling tool** allows users to plan meetings in advance and send invitations to participants. Here are some key functionalities:

- **Scheduling a One-Time or Recurring Meeting:** You can schedule a single meeting or set up a recurring session with the same Meeting ID and settings.

- **Integrating with Calendars:** Zoom integrates seamlessly with Google Calendar, Outlook, and other scheduling tools, making it easier to set up meetings with automated invitations.

- **Time Zone Adjustments:** Zoom provides automatic time zone conversions, ensuring that participants across different regions can join at the correct time.

- **Meeting Reminders and Notifications:** Notifications help ensure that attendees don't miss scheduled meetings.

2. Audio and Video Controls

Clear audio and video are the foundation of a successful Zoom meeting. The platform provides several tools to ensure high-quality communication:

- **Microphone and Speaker Settings:** Users can adjust input and output settings, select external microphones, and optimize audio quality.

- **Noise Suppression:** Zoom's built-in noise suppression helps reduce background noise for clearer communication.

- **Mute/Unmute Functionality:** Hosts and participants can mute themselves or others to eliminate distractions.

- **Video Settings:** Users can adjust brightness, enable HD video, and apply filters or virtual backgrounds to enhance their appearance.

- **Camera Switching:** On mobile devices, users can switch between front and back cameras during meetings.

3. Screen Sharing and Presentation Tools

Effective collaboration often requires sharing content, whether it's a PowerPoint presentation, a document, or a live demo. Zoom provides powerful screen-sharing tools:

- **Full Screen or Application-Specific Sharing:** Users can choose to share their entire screen or a specific application window.

- **Whiteboard Feature:** A built-in digital whiteboard allows users to brainstorm ideas visually.

- **Annotation Tools:** Both hosts and participants can use drawing tools to highlight important details on shared content.

- **Optimized Video Sharing:** When sharing a video, users can optimize it for full-motion playback and share audio from their system.

4. Chat and Messaging

Zoom's chat function enables real-time communication, both publicly and privately, during meetings. Key features include:

- **In-Meeting Chat:** Participants can send text messages, links, and files without interrupting the speaker.

- **Private Messaging:** Attendees can message specific individuals for side conversations.

- **Persistent Chat in Zoom Team Chat:** Beyond meetings, Zoom provides a persistent chat feature where teams can continue discussions asynchronously.

5. Participant Management and Engagement Tools

Keeping a meeting organized requires proper participant management. Zoom provides several tools to help hosts:

- **Waiting Room:** Hosts can control when participants join the meeting and screen attendees before allowing them in.

- **Raise Hand and Reactions:** Participants can use emoji-based reactions or raise their hands to indicate they want to speak.

- **Breakout Rooms:** Hosts can split attendees into smaller groups for focused discussions, then bring them back into the main session.

6. Recording and Transcription

Recording meetings allows participants to revisit discussions and share content with those who couldn't attend. Zoom offers:

- **Local and Cloud Recording:** Users can save recordings to their computer or to the cloud for easy access.

- **Automatic Transcription:** Zoom provides live transcriptions and captioning for accessibility.

- **Recording Management:** Hosts can set permissions to restrict who can view or download recordings.

7. Security and Privacy Settings

Security is a top priority for Zoom users, especially when handling sensitive discussions. The platform offers:

- **Meeting Passcodes and Encryption:** Hosts can secure meetings with passwords and enable end-to-end encryption.

- **Locking Meetings:** Once all expected attendees have joined, the meeting can be locked to prevent unauthorized access.

- **Host Controls:** Hosts can remove disruptive participants and disable screen sharing or chat for certain users.

8. Integration with Other Tools

Zoom is more than just a video conferencing tool—it integrates with various platforms to enhance productivity:

- **Zoom Apps and Marketplace:** Users can install third-party apps for additional functionality, such as polls, surveys, and productivity tools.

- **Integration with Project Management Tools:** Zoom connects with Slack, Trello, Asana, and Microsoft Teams to streamline workflows.

- **Collaboration with Cloud Storage:** Users can save recordings directly to Dropbox, Google Drive, or OneDrive for easy sharing.

Final Thoughts on Essential Zoom Tools

Mastering these essential Zoom tools can significantly improve your virtual communication experience. Whether you are hosting a business conference, an online class, or a casual gathering, using these features correctly ensures that your meetings run smoothly and professionally.

In the next section, we will explore some of Zoom's **advanced features** that take virtual collaboration to the next level.

Acknowledgments

Thank you for choosing *Zoom Meeting Essentials: A Step-by-Step Guide*. I sincerely appreciate your time and trust in this book to help you navigate the world of virtual meetings with confidence and ease.

In today's digital world, the ability to communicate effectively through video conferencing has become an essential skill. Whether you're using Zoom for business, education, or personal connections, I hope this guide has provided you with valuable insights and practical tips to enhance your virtual meeting experience.

I want to express my deepest gratitude to my readers—your enthusiasm for learning and growing inspires me to continue sharing knowledge. If this book has helped you in any way, I would love to hear your thoughts. Your feedback is invaluable and helps shape future editions and resources.

Finally, a special thank you to the developers and innovators behind Zoom and other virtual collaboration tools, whose work has transformed the way we connect across distances.

I wish you success in all your virtual meetings and beyond. Keep learning, keep adapting, and most importantly—keep connecting!

Happy Zooming!

www.ingramcontent.com/pod-product-compliance
Lightning Source LLC
LaVergne TN
LVHW062308060326
832902LV00013B/2110